Two Mediums

Our Guides' Views of the Afterlife

Prudence Ann Smith M.D., FACR
Contributions by Harvey Paul Karr

ISBN: 069223859X
ISBN 13: 9780692238592
Library of Congress Control Number: 2014911060
Belle Publishers, Tulare, CA

Dedication

For my eternal love and companion, my guide

As mediums, we are translating the spirits' thoughts. I am the translator. This book is yours as much as mine. In that sense, it is ours, the joint effort of two loving souls, one in spirit, the other in the physical, together. Not only have you given me the experiences that make me want to help others, you have given me the belief and faith in myself that I can. I wouldn't be who I am without you. I love you. Harvey would like to thank his guides for their loving contributions and all those in spirit who have helped him on his path.

Table of Contents

One

The Calling

There are some days when I feel that I must be one of the luckiest people on the earth to have such personal evidence and convincing experiences that my loved one is still alive and with me. This is a blessing that I thank God for, and I thank my loved ones for their support and for remaining with me on this journey.

It is a common belief among mediums who have contacted the other side that we have chosen the lives that we have, the troubles and lessons that we have, to learn from them. There are other days when I say, "How could I ever have chosen this? Was I crazy"?

We do "see through a glass dark darkly" on earth. I understand that when my time comes to transition to the other side I will see the larger picture. I will then know why my life occurred as it did and what I was supposed to learn from it, what I did learn and what I didn't learn.

Even with that knowledge, this path is a bittersweet one. The pain of loss, at least for me, never completely disappears. It becomes balanced with hope, faith, and a renewed strength to try to do better things with my life.

I read a wonderful book by Jasper Swain, "*On the Death of my Son,*" in which he relates his story. He was a lawyer in South Africa and had a son whom he loved very dearly. He lost his son through a tragic automobile accident and grief led him to seek contact with his son in a way that he would never have considered before.

He first obtained enough evidential communication through mediums to believe that his son survived death and that he was speaking with him. Eventually, he, himself, was able to communicate with his son, developing his own psychic and mediumistic abilities.

One of the major points of the book is that he finds out his son planned this life with him, knowing that his loss was the one thing that would change his father completely, and cause him to develop his spiritual side, to seek eternal rather than materialistic truths, and ultimately progress and become a better person.

In other words, his son loved him so much that he gave his own life, knowing that the loss would change his father and make him the better person that he could be.

This passage had heartfelt meaning for me, and made me come to a new understanding of the grief and loss I have had in my own life.

I discovered that there is something to be thankful for, even in the pain.

I had a relative who has passed to the other side, and, explaining things to me while he was alive, said, "Whenever you begin to feel depressed over your circumstances or bad about your own life, just go into a hospital. If you have one leg cut off and feel sorry for yourself, you will see someone who has had two legs cut off. You can always find someone else who is worse off than you. And you just might leave thinking, 'Gee, I'm better off than I thought I was.'"

You know that old saying, "The grass is always greener on the other side of the fence." When looking at other people's lives, it's easy to say, "They have it so much better than me. Look how wonderful their life is."

But when you look a little closer, you discover that they have troubles too, perhaps different from yours, but not necessarily any better. None of us escape from this life without our fair share of burdens, troubles, and heartbreak.

It's how we handle and think about those situations that makes us stronger people, better able to cope with our own problems and to attempt to help others with theirs.

I make a habit of remembering these things when I feel down. They help me make it through the rough patches.

When I look at the difficulties and pain I have been through, I realize that they have made me better and stronger, with a new resolve to pick myself up, move forward, and improve my life. I also have a new resolve to share what helped me in my journey with others who may be having similar problems.

I don't have all the answers, but I am very grateful for the help and comfort I have received from others on the earth and on the other side, for in some ways the hurt has shaped and molded me into the person I am today and the better person I hope to be tomorrow.

This book is a natural progression from my first. It is a continuation of questions I had about the afterlife. I compiled answers to a set of questions from my guides and my collaborator, Harvey's guides. They were kind enough to take the time and effort to answer my questions, in the hope that some others might find greater understanding or peace from these answers.

If you were approached by an alien, asking you what life on earth is like, what is love, what is evil, what kind of surroundings and environment do you have, what objects and scenery, what are your daily activities, work and recreation, can you imagine the breadth of answers they would get depending on who they asked?

Just as human beings are different and each would give you his or her opinion or interpretation, so spirits who once had a human body, but do not instantly become omniscient when they die, also have different outlooks, ways of explaining things, knowledge, and thought processes. They have different answers depending on who they are and where they abide.

So I have compiled their different answers and viewpoints for each question in the hope that it will diversify the answers with each individual perspective, and give the reader a broader understanding of what the spirit world is like.

This may also help to reduce individual subjectivity, which no medium can avoid, as none of us is able to translate and convey a message with 100% accuracy. If we do not do anything, whatever our career, with 100% accuracy, how can a medium, trying to transmit information from another dimension, do it with total and unerring objectivity?

Remember the telephone game kids used to play? After many transfers from one person to another, the words would get convoluted. That's with our physical ears. How much more so with our "psychic" ears?

I have grouped the specific questions into general categories and then alphabetized the categories, each as a chapter, in hope that the reader will find it easier to locate a particular topic.

Please bear in mind that the answers I present are answers I and others have heard and received, and are accepted by us on faith due to a large amount of evidential proof provided by the transmitter. They are presented for your evaluation. May you find your "own truth", as we have found ours.

Two

What a Dog Taught Me

When I wrote my first book I didn't know why I was here on earth. Now I know. It may sound strange, but a dog taught me.

Just yesterday, a woman named Pam came to my house. She was sobbing. Her dog, Daisy, a beautiful, young German Shepherd, had just passed unexpectedly. I had the good fortune to meet Daisy. She was a loving, courageous, beautiful young dog. She had been hit by a car 14 months ago on the 4th of July. She was left without the use of her hind legs, and her owner, who loved her dearly, didn't know how to make a cart to support her back legs so she could get around.

Multiple people had suggested that she put the dog down, but she took the dog to her local veterinarian for multiple surgeries, and Harvey, who is handy with building and designing things, built her a cart free of charge to support her hind legs and give her mobility. It seemed that she knew he was helping her, and he said his payment was licks, which she gave him generously.

Then, one day, Pam, the dog's owner, came to our door in grief over the loss of Daisy. Her death was swift and unexpected.

I tried to comfort Pam. My heart went out to her, not only because I had grown to love Daisy, but because I could identify with her loss and grief. I could never take her grief away, but I thought, how can I give her a small measure of comfort, a little bit of hope that this is not the end, that we will be reunited in the afterlife with our beloved friends, relatives, and pets?

I had never told her that Harvey and I were mediums, but I broached the subject discreetly and reached into the drawer and handed her a copy of my book.

I remembered how I felt when my loved one came through in that first reading from Robert Brown. I was taken from a place of darkness and despair into the light.

All of a sudden it hit me. I remembered something Robert had said to me. At the time I was in such grief I would've been happy if my life ended. He said, "You're not ready to go now, there are other people who need to witness you." I didn't know what he meant at the time. I had thought, who needs to witness me? What can I give?

But yesterday it all came together, and now I can answer that question. I can help to give some consolation to others in grief as I was consoled. That was one of the reasons I became a medium and a writer-to attempt to share the hope I was given with others on their journey through this world.

I wrote a song and I'll share the lyrics with you. It is dedicated to Daisy, the dog, and Pam, as well as all souls who are hurting from the perceived loss of a loved one.

We lose their physical presence, but the bonds of love are never severed between souls who love one another. The song is called, "Pass It On, Pass It On."

Daisy, the dog, in her brief life, taught me love and courage, and illuminated for me what my purpose is in life.

A friend of mine who is a medium was kind enough to give a reading for the dog's owner to help her in her grief. I couldn't do it because I knew too much about the dog to give her an unbiased and evidential reading. My friend's reading was as follows:

> K.'s Reading on Daisy
>
> There is a female energy associated with a dog. The dog was medium in size with cute ears and a little bit of brown around the neck. I heard the word "baby". This may either be similar to the dog's name or be because the owner treated it like a real baby.
>
> I am seeing an image of a pig, Miss Piggy. She was very pampered. She was very emotional, always looking for love. She could be loud and in your face, trying to get responses from people. She has all sorts of paraphernalia and is flamboyant but has a good heart. She could sometimes be a little bit sly, but that is just because she's always got something going.

I see saliva coming out of the corner of the dog's mouth.

I see an image of a fuzzy slipper. I also see a bottle of Skippy peanut butter with a picture of a dog on it. Do those images mean anything to you?

The dog was killed in a car accident. It was fast. It was as though the spirit was partly in the spirit world and partly here on the earth after the accident. The dog found its strength because of that. When it slept it could leave its body to go to the spirit world. This happens by going back-and-forth between both worlds.

When this dog left the earth, it was okay with going Home. It stayed around a lot longer than it needed to in order to help its owner.

It had an earlier exit point. If it weren't for you, it would have left a lot earlier.

It tried hard but didn't know how to say it. The dog didn't know how to tell the owner it was perfectly happy. She gave it everything it needed. Nothing more was needed. The dog remained here just for you and was happy to do it. It stayed here for its owner.

The dog is telling her it had certain play toys and objects and the owner worried it might not have had what it needed. The dog is saying, it wasn't about the toys, it was really about the Mom.

The dog was completely, 100% devoted to its Mom. This Mom was its world. Everything revolves around its Mom. There was a huge attachment between the two. Emphasize the word, huge.

?Was there a possible abnormal or unusual tooth? - Something weird about one of its teeth.

The dog is running around in circles going around and around. (I felt this was evidential because it reminded me of the dream the owner recently had.)

This is a very loving dog. The dog is very happy to communicate its feelings to its owner. There is a big heart connection between the dog and its owner. The heart connection is really strong. The dog is grateful that these messages are going to get to its owner.

Daisy inspired me to write a song in her memory. These are the lyrics.

Pass It On, Pass It On

Did you ever receive a gift from God
That forever changed your life?
Maybe it was a daughter or son,
A husband or a wife,
A mother or father who touched your life
And blessed your heart with joy;
A pet you loved, a lifelong friend,
A little girl or boy.

God said freely you've received,
Now you should freely give,
Give that love to other hurting
Souls, that they might live.
My yoke is easy, my burden light;
Take my burden on,
Give your loving gift to other
Souls, pass it on, pass it on.

Every time you dry a tear
Or heal a heart in pain,
Every time you touch a life
Or free a soul from shame,
Every time you lift a heart
From grief, that's fallen down,
You light a light within the world, Light a light,
pass it on, pass it on,
Give some help, pass it on, pass it on,
Change a life, pass it on, pass it on.

Three

Interesting Stories

The ICU

I had a very unique and memorable experience one day in the hospital. I was called up to do a liver biopsy on a patient in the ICU who was clinically dead. We did this as the patient was an organ donor, and the biopsy was required by law before the organ could be harvested for transplant.

As I prepared to do the biopsy, my guide, who was also my loved one, began speaking to me. He said, "Would you like to speak to the patient whose liver you are biopsying?" I was quite surprised, but said yes. I was actually having a conversation with the deceased patient during the biopsy. This was quite a profound medical experience for me, and one which I shall carry with me to the end of my physical life.

J.'s Ring

I had gone with a companion to a spirit circle in L.A. We were invited to bring along a personal item connected with someone who was deceased. I had a good friend who had lost a loved one, and thought it might help my friend to hear from them. So he gave me a ring that belonged to his loved one to take to spirit circle.

When the circle ended, it was very late and I had to get up for work the next morning with only a few hours of sleep, so I put the ring in a safe place as soon as I got home. Well, needless to say, the next evening I was out at dinner and thought of the ring. I couldn't for the life of me remember where I put it. As doubts set in I began to question myself, did I lose it? I was in such a panic that we left in the middle of dinner and headed home.

I can't even imagine how awful it would've been to go to my friend and tell him I lost the ring-the irreplaceable remembrance of his loved one. My companion came to the rescue.

The former owner of the ring came through my friend's guide and told him exactly where the ring was. As we pulled into the driveway, my friend said "Don't even get out of the car. Let me go in. I know where it is." As I was praying in the car, he came out a few minutes later with the ring.

Thank you, spirit. By the way, I did tell my friend about this horrifying episode. It was easy to laugh about it in retrospect.

Saint Dirt

I have a funny story to tell. My friends and I were at a James Van Praagh class and my friend from the medical field was mingling with other classmates when a girl came up to her to give her a reading and said, with a zoned-out look on her face, "Oh, my, you're older than dirt."

My friend began to laugh. Of course she meant my friend was an old soul, one with many previous lifetimes. But that wasn't the end. Quite a few people were wearing intentions bracelets. These are made from Swarovski crystals and worn with an intention. Most were named after Saints, archangels, or other religious or historical figures.

Someone approached my friend (the one who is older than dirt), and noticed the bracelet on her wrist. Incidentally, I had made it, as I could order the crystals, rondelles, and Bali beads from the Internet and make them for my friends free of charge. Looking at the bracelet, she asked my friend, "Oh, who is that bracelet named for"? My friend very quickly replied, "Oh, St. Dirt". I laughed like crazy and the other girl looked at her rather strangely and walked away, probably thinking, "What kind of weirdo is this"?

Kaye's Revelation

A friend in spirit circle told me about an experience that was enlightening to me. She had had a hurtful and unhappy relationship with her first husband. She referred to her second husband as the love of her life. When her first husband died, her second husband came through saying he was "showing him the ropes" of the afterlife. Her first husband came through to her to tell her that, as an atheist, he was shocked to find himself still alive after the death of his physical body.

He told her that when they divorced, it was time for them to part. He also showed her his second wife, and my friend was given the image of the other woman sitting in a house that was all dark. My friend, who is one of the sweetest and kindest individuals I know, said, "That was the first time I felt compassion for her, compassion for her pain in the death of two sons and now her husband."

So that, I believe, is the compassion we can feel for others who have hurt us, the ability to love the unlovable and the ability to understand that despite their faults, we have faults too, and their pain is not unlike ours. Perhaps this is the love that they refer to on the other side, the empathy we can feel with all souls.

Several visiting spirits in a recent Spirit Circle brought home a similar point. They were both here for a woman who was a houseguest of my medium friend, Laurie. I brought through her guest's biological father and Harvey brought through her stepfather. She was astounded, and said they hated each other in life. How was it possible they would come through for her together? We were given the understanding that each now respected the love that the other had for her. They had both put aside their differences and come through to support her. It wasn't about them, but her.

Her biological father gave me a beautiful insight. He said, "We each honor the best part of each other." How aptly said.

This Old House

I raised the question in this book of how spirits can impress their thoughts and feelings on one another and on the living. Speaking of being aware of feelings like this, many years ago I was looking to buy a house in another state. As I was looking at houses, I was shown a very nice home. It was physically attractive and newer than the home I eventually bought. But the minute I walked in I got an overwhelming feeling of depression and sadness. I just "knew" someone who previously lived there had had a very unhappy experience or life in the house. I felt it may have been alcohol or depression related, but never asked or found out. I made a b-line out of there and bought an older home, not as nice physically, but one in which I immediately sensed happiness and peace. I later found out that the previous owners had been a very happy couple who retired to a senior community.

Somehow I had known this before I was told. I felt in my soul that the previous owners of the home had been very happy and left that emotional imprint on the house. This is what they refer to as being a "sensitive" or "empath".

The Dream

I have been asking questions about love in the afterlife because some mediums say that all souls love each other equally without any special closeness. I found this difficult to comprehend and have read other texts by mediums that state that there are differences in compatibility and degrees of closeness in the afterlife.

I had a dream recently that I know was given to me as a parable by Spirit to help illustrate this subject.

In my dream I was caught up in a violent gang war. With all of the violence and shooting, I feared for my life. One of the young men in the area came over to me, put his arm around me, and led me through the turmoil, saying to other people, "This is my woman, don't bother her."

I remember thinking in the dream, "Oh there must be an ulterior motive, I expect that this person wants something in return for helping me." After we were clear of the area of violence, he simply walked off and left me to go my way.

I remember thinking, I love this soul for his kind and unselfish act. Then it dawned upon me that this was a parable or symbolic dream which was meant to show me what love is like on the other side. Spirits love each other for the kind and compassionate acts and deeds they do for others without self-motivation or expectation of reward.

Now, at last, I can understand what love is like on the other side. It is comprised of the giving acts and unselfish deeds that one soul does for another without expecting anything in return or any remuneration.

That dream has left a deep imprint on me and an understanding of the love that souls feel toward one another. I would express it as kind and unselfish deeds out of a pure and caring heart.

Why Did This Happen for Me?

I recently went to a mediumship intensive training session given by a medium in California. She was talking about healing and explained that when we look back at painful and difficult situations in our lives, we should not ask the question, why did this happen to me?

Instead, she said, we should ask the question, why did this happen for me? That takes us out of the position of being the victim, a helpless individual who cannot overcome or change the circumstances. That attitude takes away personal power and free will.

I had never looked at my own problems from that viewpoint before. It gave me an incredible new perspective on things that had troubled me.

I realize that the bad things I had experienced had not really happened to me but for me, in other words, for a learning purpose. I now ask myself what did I learn from that difficult or bad situation? What would I do if I were to encounter that situation again? What would I do to change or avoid it?

When I recognize I have learned from it, then I can cope with difficult situations in a better way and realize that I have grown as a person. Perhaps if I hadn't had that difficult situation, I would never have learned what I did, and never have grown as a soul.

My Friend's Dream

I recently had a friend who is a medium call me on the phone and tell me about a dream that she had several days ago. I always questioned myself about how accurately I am receiving messages and want to remove my own personal viewpoint or subjectivity as much as possible when I am bringing through messages from Spirit. Sometimes I get dismayed by my own shortcomings.

She told me that in her dream she was channeling a message from Spirit for me. I was somewhat uncomfortable because I was having a difficult time hearing a clear message. This certainly reflects my own insecurities and difficulties. But she went on to say that she received the most beautiful and ineffable feeling of unconditional love from Spirit toward me. They told her I had a unique and beautiful gift. Although I always struggle to be worthy of the gifts I am given, I agree that the gift of hearing loved ones in spirit is truly a beautiful and unique gift which I am ever thankful for.

This was quite a beautiful message that came to me when I needed some words of encouragement.

Guides

Guides are supposed to guide us. What does that mean? Does this mean, influence us to make sure our lives are on track regarding certain important milestones we set up for ourselves before we were born, such as meeting a future husband or wife, going to a particular school, or selecting a particular career?

Imagine if we missed one of our important choices, how that could change and affect everything else that subsequently happened to us, and possibly get us off track for our life's purpose.

Also, if the guides give us too much guidance or information, then we would have an inside track, so to speak, and never feel the consequences or weight of our personal decisions. If we were just "given" all the answers to the test, we would never learn the lesson.

So I think guides have an immense responsibility in walking a fine line between influencing us too little or too much. They must make sure we encounter the situations we planned to learn from, meet our designated milestones, but retain our free will to make the choices we learn from in the process. Harvey's guides said they impart wisdom. But our choices must be ours.

My guide states that the objectives of a guide are to keep you on track with your purpose, help you focus your energy in the right direction, and give you some counseling and wisdom if you seek it.

Cold Spots

When I was sitting on the couch in a relative's home, it was midsummer and very warm. The air-conditioner was not on at the moment. My relative was dozing in the recliner, and I was relaxing on the couch.

Suddenly, I felt an ice cold, focal pocket of air right in front of my face. It was so focal and so seemingly "abnormal", it alarmed me. I instantly reacted in fear, knowing instinctively that this was not something normal.

I had heard that spirits manifest with cold spots, but who was this? Was this my deceased mother, or a stranger? I felt fear and alarm and I began to pray. The cold spot instantly dissipated. I guess I will never know who it was, but that was my first encounter with a spirit affecting the environment.

I have since discussed the subject with mediumistic friends, who have also had personal encounters with a spirit causing temperature changes. One was discussing spirit communication with an acquaintance who was not a medium at a training class. Just as they were talking about spirit, a focal cold spot formed right between them as my friend was hearing a message from her companion's deceased loved one. They both remarked and laughed at this evidential corroboration.

Another similar type of incident occurred while I was organizing the material for this book. I had piles of paper spread out over my kitchen table and was organizing topics into sections when I suddenly had a very strong sense of someone standing behind me. I was alone in the house at the time, and it was a very uncomfortable feeling. I didn't sense that this was a loved one or someone close to me, who would have made me feel comfortable.

I have no evidential proof, such as a picture, or an EVP recording, to substantiate what I felt, but nevertheless, I felt disturbed enough to turn around, and, of course, I saw nothing. This type of feeling coming out of nowhere has actually never occurred with me before. I do suspect that it was a spirit near me, a stranger, and I now know what some of the paranormal researchers on the televised ghost shows mean when they say the hair stands up on the back of their neck when they feel a presence or an entity. I think I most likely had an encounter with a visiting spirit in my home.

Synchronicities

I have always heard lecturing mediums refer to something called "synchronicities". This is another word for "coincidences" that are likely to be more than coincidental. I have had several such coincidences lately.

I was giving a reading in a spirit circle recently when I was bringing through a spirit describing the mistakes someone in the family was making, and the turbulence those mistakes were causing. The spirit then clearly used the word "unaware". In other words, the family member was not deliberately causing discord, but they were unenlightened or "unaware", not yet insightful enough to change their approach to the situation.

The interesting synchronicity was when I encountered that same word used in the same way in Jeffrey Mark's book, "*The Afterlife Interviews*", Volume II, the very next day.

This same experience with synchronicities happened a second time. When I was preparing a title for this book, the words "team spirit" popped into my mind. The very next day I was reading Mavis Patilla's book, "*Mavis with Spirit*", and, sure enough, she used the words "team spirit" to refer to something in her book. These synchronicities did not go unnoticed and they were signposts showing me the connectedness of all things and individuals.

Spirit Communication in Dreams

I have had some visitations by loved ones in dreams. They were very vivid, very real, and I felt I was actually with the person that I loved. In those dreams I see my loved ones very clearly, what they are wearing. I can feel their emotions and touch and can hear them and converse with them word for word. These occurrences may be dreams or they may be an actual encounter in spirit, perhaps on the astral plane. In either case, they are never forgotten.

I have also had some very bad dreams. They usually consist of re-living horrible experiences I had in my life or fears associated with those experiences, and are very traumatic. They also felt very real.

One problem I have had is trying to distinguish between the two. I came to the conclusion that re-living the negative experiences in my life was a form of replaying them in my subconscious mind and trying to process them or assimilate them. The dreams I had related to fear were an attempt to overcome the fear that those negative experiences would recur. As they had such a profound effect on me, I asked my guide, are my guides giving me those dreams for some purpose, or are they a product of my subconscious mind, my own mistakes, pain, and fear? He replied that he and other guides did not give me those dreams.

I felt that was a reasonable question to ask because I have heard of other instances in which negative spirits could influence peoples' thoughts, emotions, and dreams. Since my guides were not giving me those dreams, I can conclude that either I was affected by someone negative or that my own subconscious mind was reliving bad experiences I had before and fears associated with those experiences.

I have often heard my guide speaking to me in dreams or in the relaxed mental state between full consciousness and sleep. That was always comforting, informative, and consoling. The other bad dreams were always disturbing and left me shaken. I decided that the best way to handle the recurring bad dreams, since I knew they were not being given to me by my guides for my welfare or development, was to reject them, to give them no power or validity. In that way they can no longer have a negative effect on me or influence me emotionally.

The dreams which represented visitations were always happy and peaceful and gave me comfort. I realized that I must have been sensitive even when I was young because I recall dreams like that, particularly ones in which my father was speaking to me.

Four

The Puzzling Questions

When I was asking these questions, several of the answers I got were similar to what I had read or heard from other commentators, and they left me confused.

I didn't want to present answers to you that were puzzling even to me without getting some resolution and clearer understanding of the topics. I finally received some clarification both from my own guide, and from a book I was reading that included excerpts from Charles Leadbeater's book, "*The Mental Plane*", published by the Theosophical Society, London and Benares, 1902.

My questions, and consequent interpretations are as follows.

Right and Wrong

The first question I had involves why some communicators say there are no wrong and right. I had a problem with this, because then it would logically follow that it would be all right to hurt, kill, maim, and destroy your fellow human beings. Negative behavior would be no different from positive behavior and we would live in anarchy.

A second problem I had with this statement is that many communicators refer to the earth as a school where we learn lessons, and that we attempt to progress both on earth and on the other side. The words, "lessons" and "progression", imply that there is something to learn, which in turn implies a right and wrong, and the word progress implies that there is a better goal to reach than where you are now-a progression from something worse to something better.

So finally I got some enlightenment. My guide came through a medium and said to me, Penny, you couldn't do anything wrong. Since I am far from perfect, I had to dissect the meaning of this statement. Since I'm learning lessons like all of us on earth, I'm not perfect, so what did he mean when he said I couldn't do wrong?

The way I interpret it is that whatever I do, however bad, will result in a lesson for me and therefore all the mistakes I do are not wrong, but rather a part of the learning process.

It's not that there is no wrong or right behavior. There certainly are degrees of right and wrong, because we would generally not condemn a man for defending his house or homeland if someone broke in or invaded with the intent of killing his family or taking over and destroying his country. But most people would say that killing or harming an innocent victim with malicious intent to harm is wrong. Anyone who has experienced violence or wrongful harm upon himself or his loved ones would assuredly feel that the perpetrator was wrong.

What I think my guide meant is that since the Earth is a school for learning, anything you do, whether "good or bad" by ethical or moral standards, results in a lesson and learning on your part. So there is no wrong lesson, for that's how we learn the consequences of our actions.

The concept of right and wrong does not apply to the after-life because there is no wrongful behavior on the Other Side. Because of the conditions, it can't exist.

Souls can't perpetrate wrong on each other on the other side.

1. There is no murder or physical violence because there is no physical body. You can't kill or physically harm a soul. Therefore, there can be no threat of physical injury.

2. There is no theft or robbery because there are no money or material possessions. We create the things we desire with our thoughts.

3. There are no lies, cheating, or deceit, as thoughts and intentions are known. They cannot exist.

4. There can be no misuse of sex or intimacy. Souls cannot abuse, deceive or betray one another.

5. There is no forcible domination or imposition of one soul's will upon another. All souls are free and equal and the mechanisms of domination – physical threat, dependency of one soul upon another, and money – are gone. No one is subservient to another.

6. Unhappy relationships do not exist, as those who are incompatible are not forced to remain together by legal contracts.

So no violence can exist. All the negative uses of power and control over others can't exist. All the uses of money to stratify us cannot exist. All of the enslavement of others by prejudice can't exist because all are recognized as equal. So division can't exist.

Desire to harm others physically or emotionally, to dominate, intimidate, belittle, or abuse is ineffectual. Abuse is of no effect. All power to abuse has been taken from the abuser.

There is no dependency, inferiority, or forced servitude.

Incompatible souls part ways without malice. Harmony of character, spirit, outlook, attitude, and interests draw people together. Love is like glue and knits together those who are like-minded.

So the situations and mechanisms or tools that allow one person to harm or control another on earth are non-existent in the afterlife. Those who would abuse lose the power to abuse. The abuser would find him or herself alone.

Selfishness is impotent, as there are no lies, manipulation, or deceit. No soul can be exploited by another. The motivations of profiteering are gone – financial, material, or sexual profit, or service oriented labor.

Why does this not exist on the other side? Because people's intentions and true motivations are known.

They cannot be hidden. Therefore other souls cannot be deceived. Furthermore, there is no money to enable financial profiteering. There is no need for sex to enable physical exploitation. There is no work, service, maintenance, or upkeep required for possessions, or material objects, such as homes, cars, lands, businesses, or leisure objects, so there is no ability to exploit another individual for their work or services. Also, people cannot be forced to work unfairly for the benefit of another because there is no dependency.

There is no need for the labels of "right" and "wrong" because you are unable to do wrong on the other side. So you are unable to do what we know of as wrong on earth. The opportunity isn't there.

Surely there is more love and respect on the other side when we realize that all souls are equal and that we are eternal. We are also made to realize the pain we have caused others with our words and actions in the life review. As such, we learn to control abusive and selfish behavior. We learn to consider the feelings of others, to treat others with regard, when we ourselves feel what it is like to be treated with disregard. We secede exploitative control of others, first, because we are no longer able to enact it, and, second, because we are eventually learning that it is wrong, and will no longer desire it.

It is one thing to say that we no longer kill, harm, abuse, destroy, and exploit others because we are not able to do it. It is quite another thing to say that we no longer do these things because we realize they are wrong and no longer want to do it, choose not to do it. That is what the lessons and learning are all about. How to treat others with dignity and respect, not because we have to, but because we want to. Because we choose to. In the life review, those who are abusive will feel the effects of their thoughts and actions on others.

When we are placed in an environment like the other side where we can't do it, then it is no longer a matter of our free will. When we are placed in an environment like on the earth, where we can do it, but we choose not to, then the respectful and caring behavior comes from us, from our heart, not because of the situation in which we can't do it. The lesson is that the behavior of love, harmony, and consideration should come from our heart, and not be imposed externally.

That is what we are striving for. That is what we come to earth for. To learn to govern our behavior, to treat others with the respect, consideration, and dignity with which we desire to be treated. To realize that we all are the same in the regard that we are all souls of equal value created by source. To learn to act not just in our own interest but also for the welfare and benefit of others. To practice and desire love, charity, and kindness toward others and ourselves. To realize that we all deserve it. To give it and receive it.

Illusion and Reality

Another thing that always puzzled me was the statement by some communicators that this world we live in is an illusion, and when we pass to the afterlife there is no "objective reality" and that our thoughts are our reality.

I took this to mean that they were saying we live in a dream world or fantasy world on the other side, and that no external reality existed.

Charles Leadbeater solved this dilemma for me. I was reading an excerpt from his book on the mental plane, a supposed dimension or level in the afterlife. He explained that the reason those on the other side regard this world, the earth we know, as an illusion, is because while we dwell here all we think is real is the solid reality around us, and many do not see the greater reality of the invisible world of spirit, and that all of the solid things we see around us are just a temporary reality we are living in.

We don't see the electromagnetic waves that are outside of our visible spectrum. We don't see the atoms that make up the chair we are sitting in and all the space around them. We don't see the minute processes within the cells in our bodies. Therefore, the very solid world we see is only a small part of the whole, and the fact that we think we see the whole of its reality is only an illusion.

He went on to say that we create things with our thoughts, that is, materialize them, on the mental plane of the afterlife. To an extent we do that here, also, but in a roundabout fashion.

If we want to build or "materialize" a home on earth, we start with a thought of what the finished product will look like, and this thought is translated into an architect's plans, and then "manifested" or produced by the builders who use raw materials, such as wood, man-made materials, such as bricks, mortar, nails, and screws to construct the final product. In essence, the thought has become the thing, just in a slower or more laborious manner, with more steps.

In a similar fashion, communicators say that on the mental plane, thoughts are things and produce the reality there, too, only in a more direct way, without the middlemen of the architect, manufacturers and construction workers. The thoughts manifest as things almost instantly.

So I have come to the conclusion that when some communicators say that our thoughts are our reality on the other side, it doesn't mean that we live a dream, fantasy, or hallucination. It just means that our thoughts manifest the reality about us, as they do on earth, where we construct highways, automobiles, and buildings, just more quickly and directly, without all the intermediate steps.

My collaborator, Harvey, stated it like this. "What they have on the other side is the equivalent of a CAD system here. It eliminates all the intermediate steps and errors. What we did before was to come up with a mental idea and convert it to a thumbnail sketch, submitted to a draftsman, who would come up with a conceptual drawing. And the person who came up with the individual idea would then critique it to make sure it was exactly what he had originally envisioned.

In some cases a scale mockup would be produced and critiqued and modified.

On the other side we have a pure transmission of energy where we can conceive and produce in one motion. The modification or refinement takes only a thought. You can direct or erase it with a thought. There is no waste.

It can be private or shared after you create it. It could also be a collaboration, like on earth, for the better good."

Leadbeater also suggests that on the mental plane we are aware that our thoughts project or create the reality we experience, and that, therefore, we are under less of an illusion than we are here in the physical world, where we are far less aware of the impermanence of our surroundings, the invisible forces at work, such as the atoms and smaller particles of which all things are composed, and of the invisible parts of the electromagnetic spectrum which our senses cannot detect, however real they are.

Here, we are largely unaware of the more "real" and permanent invisible spiritual world that exists outside of the limits of our sense perception.

So I understand that when some communicators say on the other side that our thoughts create our reality, it doesn't mean that we are just experiencing a hallucination. It means that our thoughts directly influence our environment and create the conditions around us, and those conditions are not a delusion, but are real to us as the chair I am now sitting in and the table next to me that holds my iced tea and cell phone.

F.W.H Myers, purportedly communicating from the afterlife through the medium Geraldine Cummins, commented that when we are on earth we only see a small portion of the greater reality. "Therein lies the unreality of the temporal world."

I included these two discussions because these are issues that troubled my logical mind, and I wanted to resolve them to the best of my understanding. I may not learn the lessons I have come here to learn any quicker, but at least I will comprehend them to the best of my ability.

The Me versus My Reincarnated Selves

There are books and mediums who have discussed the concept of an oversoul, a supposed energetic portion of ourselves that remains in the afterlife while only a portion of our total energy contributes to each incarnational individual.

That oversoul supposedly stores the information from our many previous incarnations. It was difficult for me to conceive of the various selves I supposedly have been in my prior lives on earth.

This led me to think about what makes me an individual and who I am inside. If I have had prior lives as a male, a member of the different nationality or race, with a different occupation and different family, what makes me "me"? What specifically is the personal identity that I would carry with me through reincarnations as multiple different people?

I reflected on this subject and these are the answers I came up with.

There is a core me that feels, thinks, and has a unique identity, that is, a unique emotional personality, a type within its variations and fluctuations, with individual thoughts, as well as a world outlook consisting of opinions, values, and preferences. My nature also includes preferences, likes and dislikes, and opinions about the greater reality of being and the world and environment around me. These feelings, thoughts, preferences and opinions make up my unique identity, and this being that I am is thrust into this life and conditions to act, feel, and learn from the circumstances. I grow and modify myself, my being, in that way.

I am the same "me" whether I am born a man or woman, born into a particular nationality, a particular language or society. I am expressing and playing different roles, rich, poor, mother, father, brother, sister, husband, wife, child, or experiencing different circumstances, occupations, languages, careers, hobbies, interests, recreations.

All of these are experiences of my soul, from which I learn and grow. But they are the input, the experiences that I have. They are not the me, the intelligence, the core being that is sensing and integrating these experiences.

I am capable of experiencing these various external roles and situations, of choosing actions in the various situations I encounter. I am an intelligent, sentient being at the helm of this physical vessel I currently inhabit.

My unique feelings, thoughts, and preferences determine my actions and make me "me". Whatever clothing I put on, whatever role I play, I am me. The role as an English speaking female physician in California is like a set of clothing that I currently wear, a role I currently play. When I die I pull off that role and realize I can come back and try another set of clothing, another role. But the roles aren't fixed. I may be a caregiver or child bearer and alternatively an income provider in the same lifetime. I may be a technical writer and a physician in different parts of that same lifetime.

The roles are changing but the me behind them is the same, just growing and learning as a result of what I do and what happens to me, as a result of my experiences and actions. I realize these roles are ephemeral and have blurred or indistinct boundaries. I form and create. I map a unique course, a unique pattern within the fabric of existence. My thoughts, choices, and actions, whatever circumstances I am in, create my world around me.

The remainder of the book addresses various questions with answers provided by our guides. They offer varying viewpoints and ways of addressing each topic. They are arranged in alphabetical order rather than order of importance, for easier access.

Five

Healing Negative Thoughts and Behavior Patterns

In Jeffrey Marks' book, "*The Afterlife Interviews*", Vol. II, he describes two things available to spirits on the other side that we don't specifically have on earth.

One of these is help groups that enable a soul to view their personal thoughts or behavioral patterns that limit them and prevent them from moving forward, and help them to "re-program" those negative habits and thought patterns by re-living them from a positive standpoint and changing them.

I realized that my guide has been doing this with me. I had some repetitive emotionally traumatic events in my life that have led me to feel "trapped" in those same scenarios, to feel that I expect them to happen again, that they will repeat, and that I am not worthy to experience something better or receive better treatment.

By giving me emotional support, he has enabled me to "re-live" the negative experiences, but now with positive treatment from him and a positive outcome. This has enabled me to release the fear and expectation of the same negative treatment and cyclical pattern occurring, and to feel that I don't have to continually re-live the same harmful predicament. I now feel that I have an inner value and no longer have to be mistreated or demeaned by others.

I am now re-living or changing the past negative events by living a new similar circumstance and relationship, but this time in a positive and beneficial way, with happiness as the outcome. This re-programs or re-trains my soul to believe in, accept, recognize, and author positive results for myself.

I am not changing what happened, but changing my intention and what I would do now if I had to relive those experiences. I am also creating and living a current new experience that is positive, not negative as my past experiences were.

In that way I am breaking the negative pattern and replacing it with something much better. I am healed of the pain associated with the past. I no longer expect those negative situations to continually occur, and feel that I am worthy to experience positive situations instead.

Does the pain remain? Yes, if I think about those former experiences, but I no longer feel "trapped" or compelled to experience or relive them in the future.

Six

Projecting and Creating Your Future

Another thing the spirits in Jeffrey Marks' book, "*The Afterlife Interviews*", Vol. II, refer to as being available on the Other Side is the ability of spirits to learn to control energy and make projections for the future experiences and growth of their souls.

I realized that my guide is helping me to do that as well. We make positive plans and declarations for our future. We discuss our outlook and desires, coordinating and unifying them as a team. We "speak them into reality" with our intentions and make daily positive affirmations with one another.

This has helped me tremendously to compromise and coordinate our relationship and plans, to unify as distinct but united souls on a path linked together.

Seven

Addiction

How do people with addictions rehabilitate on the Other Side? Does being an addict in your earth life cause any effects in the afterlife when you cross over?

A friend who is a medium and psychologist told me that, to her surprise, spirits who suffered addictions while they were on earth do, as a rule, take longer to "normalize" or recover in the afterlife. Effects of the addiction seem to last for a while.

My Guide:

> We don't have instant recovery. If we have had a problem that has been a deeply ingrained problem or a long dependence, we may cling psychologically to that problem. There is no physical need but psychological addictions or deep needs may not be overcome instantaneously.

They may require a longer period of time to resolve, and the mental or psychological impressions or needs may inhibit development until resolved.

Harvey's Guides:

When you cross over, you cross over as you are, and it takes time to regenerate.

Eight

Advanced Levels

Are there advanced levels and what are they like?

My Guide:

There are many advanced levels.

No one who hasn't been there can understand it in its entirety. If you think of all the good things you have ever hoped for-not fleshly, but spiritual-that is the fabric and atmosphere of other elevated levels.

If you think of how you would like to be treated, that is the social interaction at those levels. If you think of the best you can be, you have a small glimpse of the kindness, beneficence, and love that is had by all in such an environment. That heaven is within you when you put on those attributes of God.

Harvey's Guides:

Advanced levels are very similar in appearance to the lower levels but with the opportunity for more advanced learning. It is like walking through a river to cleanse yourself. You have the opportunity to throw off your mistakes, imprint the learning you brought with you from the earth plane, and throw off past mistakes.

We still retain the ability to not repeat those mistakes. We need less earthly remembrances. We retain our earthly learning and the best of ourselves.

Nine

Advice

What advice would you give to those of us still in human form?

My Guide:

Live in peace with others as much as possible. Practice helpful kindness. Respect yourself and others. Teach and learn. Don't permit others to harm you and seek not to harm others. Protect yourself and do not seek to harm others.

Harvey's guides:

Live every day like it's your last. Leave no stone unturned. Hold out a hand of friendship.

Guides come and go. You have different guides at different times in your lifetime. Guides are just a conduit. We are less important.

Is there any message you would like to leave me with?

My Guide:

We need to be careful with our desires, because what we desire becomes manifested for us. We have the power of creation, and what is our heart's desire becomes our reality. You and I will have our own.

Please give me your thoughts on making good choices.

My Guide:

Part of the problem in life is learning to make appropriate choices. That is, how to distinguish between a good alternative and a bad alternative. This involves experience and discrimination - applying the experience you have had, incorporating it into the wisdom to make more informed choices.

You must also gain the understanding to not let your previous poor judgments and choices make you gun shy and afraid to commit to a good choice. You must first try the experience, look for signs, observe and interpret wisely, and then not be afraid to embrace what is good.

Knowing what actions led to what results in the past helps you to avoid unproductive behavior in the future. Once you gain greater insight, you will be able to make more beneficial choices and live a better life. Learning is a process that is never finished. We are always presented with new experiences and opportunities. Learning to take advantage of the ones that lead us to our own happiest outcome is the gift of wisdom gained from life.

It is only by the cost of our mistakes that we learn. Also, what is right for one person is not necessarily right for another. We are dealt a hand of cards in life, and as the Kenny Rogers song said, "You got to know when to hold 'em and when to fold 'em.

Ten

Afterlife Environment

What do spirits look like in the afterlife?

My Guide:

You and I will have a similar appearance to what we had on earth. You and I will both look like we did. We do have more than one appearance. We all have our own choices.

We can look like we did on earth with a similar kind of outward form or we can appear as a form of light, a mist, or an orb. We are able to change our appearance at will. We don't have to have a set appearance or look any particular way. We are able to look as we wish. We are able to change our forms and appearance.

We all have our own preferences and can assume a humanoid or energetic form or change back-and-forth. Most of us will choose to look like we did on earth. We have more of those who will choose to assume a form like they had on earth.

We have more freedom when we are in spirit form. We have more opportunity to move around easily and freely. We have more flexibility and the limitations of movement are less. We are not bound by the earthly physical laws of movement. We are able to travel in different directions and at different speeds.

Some of us prefer to maintain a more physical form in order to have a relationship more like the one we had on earth. Our perspectives are different and influence our choices. If we choose to keep a more physical form we can act in a manner more like we did on earth. If we choose to keep a more physical-like form we can do things like kiss, hold hands, and hug.

We can act and move like we did on earth. We can laugh, dance, even sing if we want to. We can create the songs to sing or talk if we desire. We don't need the vocal apparatus. We can create sounds with our thoughts. We can create movement with our force, or energy. We create things with our thoughts.

We can create bodies and make movements as we would have on earth. We can make more inventive dance movements than we would have on earth as the Spirit body is more flexible, less rigid. We can create similar environments, situations, and appearances to those we had on earth.

We can create sports, too, if we wish. We are able to create all activities on earth and more. We do not have the negative or harmful aspects of those activities.

We are able to create environments similar to those we had on earth both in terms of nature and man-made structures. We do have some environments that are more set and stable and others we are able to influence. We create our own environment to a certain extent. We are able to make an environment with our thoughts, desires, and wishes. We can create some things that are similar to our Earth experiences.

We do have matter and substance but it is more under our control then the substance and matter on earth. It is more easily manipulated. We are in an environment where we have more opportunities to create and control.

Is there a common reality that everyone sees or does each soul have its own subjective reality?

My Guide:

We have some realities that are more complex than others. We have common realities already created and in existence and can superimpose our own manifestations upon that reality. We don't have the same restrictions as we do on earth. We have nature and structures/buildings.

We have common realities that souls create with the objective of enjoying them. We can make our own more subjective realities if we wish. We can design our own type of environment for ourselves.

Your imagination is your limit. You have more appearances, realities, designs than you can imagine. There are less limitations on our ideas so our creations are even more fanciful. The possibilities seem endless. Earth is more structured and bound by physical law.

The material where we exist is changeable, subject to influences readily, and more easily altered. You are able to imagine things and they come true.

For instance, what if someone wanted a car or a motorcycle ride or a hot air balloon trip or a boat ride? Can you have it?

We create the situation with our thoughts and it becomes reality to us. We can create an image of a car and objectify that car, place ourselves in that scenario or situation and re-create the experience of a car ride. It appears real to us and our experience of it feels real.

We can create and experience the realities of our imagination-our fantasies. We have more options here than we ever had on earth. We can create the sensation of eating or of sex. We don't have it in a way that is analogous to the Earth way but we experience the feeling of it. Although we don't have the same mechanism or means/apparatus, and it is not achieved in the same manner or with the same modus operandi, the experience feels the same. The end result, the apprehension is similar to that on earth although created or achieved in a different manner.

Colors are very beautiful, music more intense. All beauty, all sensory experiences are heightened. They are more sophisticated or elegant forms of the earthly.

We are not in love with the earth. We are content here unless we miss the grosser sensations or the cruder physical habits. These are replaced by more elevated sensations, more elegant gratifications.

We are not in a prison. We have very different ideas of what we choose, our desires, interests and paths. We are divided by these-by our tastes and objectives.

We have more love and kindness, more understanding of our feelings and those of others and more helpfulness. We can experience anger but don't have the same provocation. We are not able to harm, cheat, steal, or practice the earthly vices, and as such are much more at peace. We interact more pleasantly with others. We grow at our own pace.

We seek our own. If we have discordant or contrasting personalities we do not remain with or spend much time with those souls. We spend time with like-minded souls, in harmonious relationships. We spend time with those who are similar in thought, nature, and emotion.

Like attracts like and we associate with those with whom we have a warm bond of affinity and the deepest love. Where there is not deep love and affinity we don't spend much time.

People who are dissimilar or inharmonious or have very different personalities, mindsets, and goals part ways. Those of a similar nature, tastes, and goals, remain close.

Those who have a true affinity and the deepest bonds of love remain together.

There are some who never want to part. There are those who express a spiritual commitment to one another to remain together for eternity. They are rare but not unheard of.

Does the afterlife environment have any of the familiar things of the earth or is it something so different we can't even imagine it? What are conditions and scenery like in the afterlife?

My Guide:

We have some things that are similar to the earth. We have a semblance of things on earth in a different medium. We have very different materials but similar concepts. We do have buildings and the scenery that we had on earth. We have nature – hills, lakes, trees, mountains, plains, forests, all of the things in nature. We have buildings, some of unique design, some replicas of those on earth. All the things that you can imagine on earth we have.

We do have structure. We are not formless, nor do we live in a formless environment. We have more items than we have on earth. Some things are more variations of the earthly things, embellishments of the earthly things, and some are entirely original. You can't even begin to imagine what we have here. It's more of a fantasy makeup – things that can't be constructed on earth.

We have some things that are the product of imagination, more advanced. We all have some type of scenario we prefer. We can inhabit that scenario. We are limited only by the constructs of our imagination.

It's like those on earth who have a different reality – those who live in the wilderness in a cabin and those who live in a penthouse in New York City.

We manifest our desires and predilections. We are able to create with our thoughts the reality we desire. We do have places that are reminiscent of the earth and others that are novel. We have no limits except those we impose.

We can have buildings. We can have nature. We have all different types of settings. If we want to create our environment, we can. We also have fixed environments that others have created.

We have materials that are more influenced by our thoughts than we have on earth. We interact with our environment. We can create things similar to what we had on earth if we want them. If we live in a place similar to the earth, we create things similar to what we are familiar with.

We can make a structure as we wish it. It's like a great masterpiece that we create with our imagination- not as rigid, more easily developed by our thoughts. We do have places that have things similar to the earth, such as water, trees, mountains and such. We have locations that are similar.

Harvey's Guides:

Are there trees, water, and buildings? Is there nature and construction? If you want it. There can be, but there doesn't have to be. You can have whatever you want. It is up to the individual. What you want you will have.

There can be nature and buildings, but it doesn't have to be in the same manner as it was on earth. It can be different. There are more options. We do have the things you have on earth, but there are also many more things you can experience in the afterlife that are unlike the things of the earth.

If there was something you wanted all your life on earth and you never got it, you will have it in the afterlife.

What is the afterlife environment like? Can you visualize anything? Are there objects? Is there nature? Or are you a formless blob of energy floating in endless darkness?

My Guide:

We don't inhabit a lonely dark isolated world living without sensation. We don't live like an energy floating in space with nothing around it.

We can create the equivalent of things we had on earth if we want to. We can create the reality we want and live in it.

We can see, but not with the same senses we had on earth. We have a different sense that allows us to see things and interpret them. They are energy forces and I interpret the waves that come into my energy field. I can "see" or get visual images but not the same way you see them.

When I asked if there are exterior objects in the spiritual world, I was told, we created buildings on earth, we can create them here too.

Asked whether there are trees and water I was told, there are all kinds of landscapes available and we can create our own.

Yes, we can do activities like we did on earth. We can do the things that are similar to what we did on earth.

We create our own visualized version of what we wish. We create a thought. It comes to life. And we experience it. It feels real to us.

Harvey's Guides:

It can look like anything you considered. Realities are individual. Some spirits keep together. These are like-minded people. You can have a collective reality.

As on earth, if you don't like where you end up, you can move. You find your own utopia. Similar energy draws together.

Can we have houses in the afterlife?

My Guide:

We can have them if we wish them. Most people who have our type of mentality want them. We have the option of making a home if we want it. We have many who wish them. Most of those who have the same type of thought process as you and I will have a home. We can have one. All of us have our own preferences.

Are there any enjoyments of the soul that are unlike anything we have experienced on earth?

My Guide:

We have more enjoyments than we ever had before. These are beyond anything we experienced on earth. We have more acute and intense music, more readily available learning and understanding, heightened positive emotions, more beautiful surroundings, colors, and visions.

We are not limited by the range of our earthly organs of perception. We have all the beautiful sensations of Earth intensified, expanded, and escalated. We have inner peace and joy not readily achieved on earth. We live in an atmosphere of love and tranquility. We have the joy of the knowledge of eternal life, of the presence of purpose, and of a divine creator.

We are more content and fulfilled. We reach greater heights of accomplishment.

Also, we have enjoyments that are beyond physical description as a computer or cell phone would be to a man in the Stone Age.

We can live in a scenario we create. We can produce and instantly share ideas, feelings, visions, images, and thoughts and stories. Whatever we create and visualize in our imagination can be perceived and felt by others, as long as the intent is not to harm.

We are the embodiment of creativity. We also have sensations and understandings, feelings for which there is no analogy or equivalent on earth.

More than once I have asked myself, "If there are some contradictions between things I read in books or what another medium said, am I wrong"? Maybe I'm not a good enough medium and I'm interjecting my own thoughts into the message.

My Guide:

If the answer is that there are many answers, that is an answer in itself. We have all good things like the earth. We have trees, mountains, water, all things of nature, modern and ancient forms of architecture. We have ground and sky. We can manifest cars and roads for our pleasure but do not need them. We can create homes, but they are not necessary. They are a matter of choice and desire. We have groups of souls who come together for the purpose of learning and can have buildings or "schools" to that effect.

Harvey's Guides:

No, what is true for one spirit is not necessarily true for another. There are many "realities" and you experience your own. You have what is true for you and that may not be true for another. If one person says one thing and another says another, it isn't that one is right and the other wrong. Both are true. That is why there are so many different answers when we ask questions about the afterlife. Even guides have different opinions.

Eleven

Age in the Afterlife

When someone who is old passes over, do they immediately look young again as they would have at the prime of their life, or do they age backwards gradually?

My Guide:

We can let go of the past very quickly and return to our youth. It depends on the soul. It's up to the individual soul. Each has his period of readjustment. Some will take longer than others.

Lameness, sickness, and other disabilities are cured instantly. But we all need time to mentally adjust to the new environment. We need time to work out issues and deep scars, to learn our purpose in life and digest our life review.

Some are not able to readjust as quickly as others, depending on their thought patterns, expectations, and values, their degree of spirituality and development. There are others who are a quick study.

Once I realized I was able to change my appearance I became young quickly. We come out in a finer replica of our human body. We can regress to an earlier period of time and appearance. We can do this right away if we wish to. Most souls often do it after a short period of time.

Most often we change very soon. We have no need to stay in an old appearing body. Sometimes it's more gradual, but it doesn't have to be.

Harvey's Guides:

I think that's subjective. Some older people, with all of their knowledge and experiences, are at their prime. Look at Einstein, with all of the knowledge he had gained in his lifetime.

Question: At the time of your death when you first left your body did you leave in a replica of your physical body as it appeared at that time?

Yes and no. At the time you are preparing to leave your body the difficult and painful things you had to encounter are lifted from you. Sickness, trials, and tribulations are seen for what they really are-trivial.

A physical body is less important to you after you transition than what it was on earth. The physical doesn't have the same importance. There is so much to learn in the afterlife it would get in the way.

Question: when you cross over, if you choose to have a semblance of a human form, do most souls choose to look as they did in the prime of their life?

They have a choice. Some prefer to appear in their teens, 20s. Others, especially if with their twin flame, could be in their 70s if they grew old together. It depends on the individuals and what they deem important. There is no rubberstamp answer.

It depends on what they felt was the most important part of their life. Being with each other was the most important thing, not how they looked.

Twelve

Aliens

A friend of mine who is a medium has channeled soul groups such as Silver and Abraham. Some of the members have not had earth or human incarnations. Their messages are always loving and inspiring, but it is interesting to note that when my questions involve human things, like houses, eating, and romantic love, they do not entirely relate to those concepts because they did not have human lives. One member of Silver responded to my question about food by saying, "Who would ever want to eat"? When I asked if we could hug or kiss in the afterlife, they said, "Romantic love is a human emotion".

I am not saying this to disparage those soul groups. They are loving, generous, and altruistic souls, and kind enough to allow me to pester them with my questions. But that experience taught me that values and experiences in the afterlife vary among souls and are personal.

Just as I wouldn't ask someone who lived in downtown Manhattan all their life about how to survive in the Alaskan wilderness, so I would approach souls who had previous human lives to ask them about things that are relevant to humans.

It is a fact of life that we have certain things in common with some souls and not others. Recently, when I was having some difficulties, my mediumistic friend passed on a very loving and supportive message to me from those soul groups. I was very touched and learned from that experience that there is one thing we can all have in common that unifies us – love.

Are there some of us who are alive on the earth now who have been aliens before?-That is, have had lives on other planets, galaxies or dimensions?

My Guide:

Some of us who have lives as humans on earth have had incarnations in different dimensions. We all have different evolutional paths. Our paths intersect for a time and then diverge. Some of us have had a lifetime in a different dimension.

Most of us have had many lives, some more than others. We have lived in different areas, inhabited different bodies, and experienced different genders and races. None of us have had identical experiences. More often than not we have not had just one life but many. We are not limited or linked to any one experience.

There are souls here who have never experienced incarnation in a physical environment while others have experienced lives in another part of the universe.

Most of us have had lives in a different place, time, and body on the earth. Some have had lives outside of the human experience.

Have any of those currently living on earth ever incarnated elsewhere, such as another planet, world, or galaxy?

My Guide:

Yes, there are souls that have incarnated in places other than the earth.

Harvey's Guides:

Quite possibly. With all of the billions of planets it's not sensible to think that there is no other intelligent life.

In the afterlife, the differences in people are insignificant. White, black, short, tall, skinny, fat, none of it counts.

What does count?

Purity, pure thoughts, pure actions.

Thirteen

Angels

Are there angels and if so, what are they?

My Guide:

Angels are beings created for a specific task, to be the mediators between God and humanity. We have some who have been human before and reached a similar level of development.

Harvey's Guides:

There are angels. They are developed or advanced souls who help those who are less evolved.

Fourteen

Annihilation

Are there any souls that are ever eradicated or erased and re-processed by God or reissued?

My Guide:

No. We can say that they destroy themselves because they refuse to accept change, to seek higher. They are self-satisfied and unwilling to alter themselves. They are inflexible and vain-feeling that they are right, never wrong. They choose darkness over light.

They are more blind than a blind man, more deaf than a deaf man, for they are spiritually deaf and blind. They only have to ask for help and be willing to change and they will be given help. But they first must realize that they need to change. It is an awareness problem. Stubborn ego is often to blame.

No one is going to eradicate us. Our progress is of our own making. We have to be willing to learn if we want to progress. We can remain in a negative state indefinitely if we refuse to change or progress. Souls that are extremely negative are in a different place and cannot influence those on higher levels. They are not a threat to those who are more developed.

They live in a very unhappy state in a negative environment. They don't have the same opportunities those have who are more advanced. They are not destroyed by God, but themselves destroy their own inner light. No, they are not re-programmed. They are lost in their own inner emptiness, dead to the light. They are prisoners of their own negativity, and the happiness and love of the higher levels evades them.

Harvey's Guides:

No. Spirits that choose to ascend learn from their prior transgressions. The difference is how long it takes on each level. If they're willing to learn they will ascend. If not, they'll stay on a lower plane.

Fifteen

Astral Travel

Do we astral travel and leave our bodies at night to join others who have passed previously to Spirit?

My Guide:

> We are able to contact the spirit world more easily when we are in a state where the conscious mind is not as active. We achieve this in sleep, and can have more ready discourse with Spirit. We can astrally project, but do not have to leave our body for this communication.
>
> Some do travel astrally, some are more capable than others, and those who do have more intense communications.
>
> Some dreams are reliving our fears, sometimes from a past life. Those are not visitations. Visitations are the very vivid dreams from a loved one sensed as a real event.

Harvey's Guides:

Occasionally. It's not an everyday occurrence. Most of us don't remember our dreams. The most vivid dreams are usually visitations with our loved ones.

When we have bad dreams, it's not necessarily our past. It can be things we have heard or disasters we fear that may affect us. This might also be tied into memories of past lives, but such memories hopefully enable us to avoid repeating the trauma.

The ones you remember are usually contacts with your loved ones. We only remember a tiny percentage of our dreams. If you have a bad dream, it could be that you are repeating a fear from your childhood which has become a paranoia.

Sixteen

Baggage

How would you define baggage?

My Guide:

Baggage is unresolved issues from the past that do not allow you to focus and move forward.

Seventeen

Behavior

I have heard it said that the way you do one thing, is the way you do everything. Can you shed some light on that comment?

My Guide:

Your moral character pervades every aspect of your life. You take the same philosophical approach to all the decisions you make. Your guiding principles direct every aspect of your life. Your convictions drive your choices. Our choices are a product of our understanding and our viewpoint.

Harvey's Guides:

Behavior is a product of our personality, which is usually consistent.

Eighteen

Bilocation

Can souls be in two places at once?

My Guide:

We can divide our energy and be in several places at once. It's like multitasking, where a part of our attention is devoted to one thing and a portion of our awareness or energy to another. It's difficult to do, but we can learn to do it.

Not all souls choose to do it. We are capable of doing it. We can have different things going on at once. No one I know just lives that way continuously. It is a state we can assume temporarily for efficiency and then we resume our normal condition again. Those I know can do it sporadically, temporarily, for a reason and then coalesce their energy into one unit again.

We can also communicate from a distance with our thoughts without dividing or transporting our energy.

Harvey's Guides:

Yes, we can divide our attention or energy. It depends on how advanced we are.

Nineteen

Children

When children die young and cross over to the afterlife do they instantly revert back to the soul that they were before they came to earth or do they have to grow up so to speak in the afterlife?

My Guide:

They can come back and go back to what they were before as long as they are aware of what they have been through. They can go back right away to being who they were in the afterlife, but they all have some period of adjustment.

They come back with the mindset of a youthful person. They don't require very much time but they can take time to adjust if they want. They often choose to live as a young soul for a while until they are acclimated.

It really depends on who they were before they went to earth. They need to be reintegrated. Those in their circle of soul friends help them readjust their lives.

It normally takes only a short period to resume their normal identity. Souls don't have an exact age so they readjust themselves and prepare to become the soul they were before they came to earth.

So it depends on how they see themselves and how rapidly they adjust. Young people take some adjustment and often stay at a younger age for a while until they are re-oriented. When they become more aware of who they were they can then change.

Harvey's Guides:

I think they have the opportunity to stay young. Sometimes young souls have completed their mission on earth. I think the point of remaining young is the need of the people they left behind. It depends on how much they are needed by those they left behind. They can stay young in their mind because that's how they'd be remembered.

Twenty

Compassion

Recently I was reminded of the importance of the small gestures of love. I have always been interested in the variations of love, agapeic, filial, brotherly, romantic, unconditional, etc. Two mediums I know have said that we are all together and we all love each other equally on the other side, and I used to think, does that mean we would spend an equal amount of time with all those on the other side or love them all equally?

For instance, does that mean we would love a physically abusive boyfriend or the man who molested and murdered our child as much as we love a husband who was the deeply loving companion of a lifetime, or a mother who was always there for us?

I can understand that perhaps we are meant to forgive those who have done us wrong or make peace with those with whom we have had negative relationships, but do we really love everyone the same, or are we equally close with every other soul in the afterlife?

One soul quoted in Jeffrey Marks book, "*The Afterlife Interviews*," helped me to understand this seeming dilemma. That soul stated, "They always talk about how we all love each other in the afterlife. What it really means is that we service each other on our journeys."

Well, this has always been a puzzle in my mind and the other day spirit gave me the answer. I was reading patient studies when I was called out to speak with a mother and her son, who had had a study read by another physician. She explained that her son was very concerned about the results. Would it be possible for me to review the films with them? Even though I was busy I invited them back into my office. After I reviewed the films with them and discussed the results, I also discussed some of the problems the young man was having, as some of my family members had had similar problems.

When the mother rose to depart, she shook my hand and said something that made the subject clear as day in my mind. She said "You don't know how much you have helped this soul by taking the time to discuss these things with him." It was the way she said it. Suddenly everything became clear. The love they speak about in the afterlife is compassion, consideration for other souls, and willingness to help where we can. Finding peace, finding forgiveness, the kind of love that I believe God has for us. It doesn't mean that we cease to be individuals and no longer have the special bonds with those we loved deeply in this life, or that it's all the same to us whether we're with someone we were deeply devoted to our entire lifetime or with the criminal who just hacked up 10 people and buried them in his basement. Does it mean you will love or be just as close to a heartless selfish in law as to the young son you adored and lost?

I have been told that some souls are closer and do have a deeper love for one another than others. But the love we have for all souls is not so much the love that makes us want to be together, but the love of service to others, of kindness and compassion.

Twenty One

Contacting Spirits/ Loved Ones

Can we contact anyone in the afterlife when we think of them? Can they hear us?

My Guide:

It depends on their knowledge about communication and their availability. The veil is difficult to pierce and if there is a strong love connection, it can be bridged.

Yes. We can hear your thoughts, thoughts which are directed to us with strong feeling.

Harvey's Guides:

We can't always contact someone because they may be busy, or when someone crosses over it takes a while for them to learn to come through by lowering their vibration and for us to raise ours.

Twenty Two

Creation

Are there old souls and new souls?

My Guide:

Souls are in various stages of development. Some have had more incarnations than others. Some learn or progress more quickly than others. Some were created earlier, and some later. We are always seeing new souls emerging. There is truth to the expression, "He or she is an old soul."

Harvey's Guides:

Souls are being created endlessly. Some are new souls, and some old souls. That's why we have déjà vu and savants.

Twenty Three

Crossing Over/ Loved Ones

Do we see our loved ones and do they help us cross over when is our time to die?

My Guide:

Yes. We can greet our loved ones when they are dying. We can come to help them cross over.

Harvey's Guides:

We can come to help and comfort our loved ones when it is time for them to cross over.

Twenty Four

Death

Is there such a thing as dead people who don't know they're dead?

My Guide:

Many of the dead who remain near the earth do know they're dead. Some of them can be confused as they continue to think as an individual and not realize they have passed on.

Harvey's Guides:

They are in familiar surroundings and they don't reason the same way we do. Time doesn't exist, and the things that were important to them on the earth are no longer important, such as eating and elimination habits. They can be trying to contact the living and not know they're dead.

What does death feel like? Do we lose consciousness or remain conscious through the process?

My Guide:

A surrender. A release to the powers that control the voyage of the soul. I lost consciousness briefly and then became aware of my surroundings again. I was greeted by loved ones, but then went through the tunnel into the light.

I received all the memories I had of my lifetime. I was guided through some reorientation and I was given a life review. It was difficult. I saw where I made mistakes and felt how others responded to me.

I talked with others in my lifetime and discussed things with them. We are able to communicate with our thoughts, so we get in touch with others that we love easily.

We can't go somewhere we are not suited to go for reasons of our development. We have many places we can go, very few restrictions.

Harvey's Guides:

It feels like a release from all the trials and tribulations of your life- like you're floating and leave all your problems behind you. It is a final euphoria.

There is no one single answer. For some, they actually see their loved ones coming for them. For some, it's just a final release and relief from pain. We do keep a vestige of consciousness.

When we cross over is it fearful?

My Guide:

It's not fearful. We need time to acclimate. We've been away for a while and have to resume our life here.

We are more at peace than those on the earth. It's much more loving. We live in an atmosphere of loving kindness. We don't have fear.

Harvey's Guides:

No. There is nothing to fear. You'll leave that behind. Everyone who has an out of body experience relates it to utter peace and no fear. They have no reason to exaggerate.

Can we influence the time of our own death?

My Guide:

The time of our death and means of our death is planned by us in the afterlife. We can influence it to a degree. If we lose the will to live, our body can sicken, or if we feel we have an important task to accomplish, we can extend our time to a degree. For the most part, we adhere to the schedule we planned.

How far ahead do we know the time of our death?

My Guide:

We do make provisions for our future lives in the after-life. We do know when, where, and how we will die. We also have some leeway based on our life and choices, but we most often adhere to the schedule we planned.

We can to some extent hasten our demise or extend our lives by our own will. We have some flexibility.

The soul knows when it is going to leave. It depends on our degree of sensitivity and our desire to know or our need to know whether or not we will be consciously aware of it. We can have an intuitive knowledge if we wish to "straighten out our affairs" before we go.

Some of us are very aware that our departure is close at hand. It can be an instinctual knowing of the soul and it depends on our sensitivity as well as our desire or need to know.

Twenty Five

Demons

Are there demons that are non-human negative entities?

My Guide:

Yes, there are demons, but demons were not created. They were in the spiritual realms and chose a darker path. All creatures can change if they wish. Those who don't, have their own dark plane of their own creation that they inhabit.

Harvey's Guides:

There are non-human spirits and they can be negative or positive. Many negative spirits are people who were negative in their lifetime.

People permit them to have power and contribute to their influence. There are negative and positive spirits that exist, and sometimes people call them demons.

Yes. Just as there are good people who go astray there are angels who can choose wrong. No one is perfect. There are good people who do bad things, and bad people who can do some good things.

Laurie's Guides:

Yes, there may be something we would equate with demons. However, we don't give them credence as acknowledging them gives them power.

Twenty Six

Desires

Can we experience something in the afterlife that we may have wanted all of our life on earth and never attained? How do we achieve the desires we have on the other side?

My Guide:

Your wish creates the behavior that will help you attain it. We draw our own circumstances to us by our wishes, thoughts, and desires. We create our circumstances more directly than we do on earth. We eliminate the middleman.

On earth we have to plan for and fund an education, look for romance and dating, conceive of ideas for buildings and locate materials to use, and then execute the project. In the afterlife we can materialize situations or environments with our thoughts.

Laurie's Guides:

A lot of the things that you wanted to accomplish but may not have been able to accomplish in your lifetime, you can accomplish on level three of the afterlife. Level III is most like the earth plane.

Twenty Seven

Discrepancies

One problem I have had in my quest for information about the afterlife is the discrepancies between the answers for any given topic in the various published books.

To give you an example, I wondered, do spirits still have a liking for food in the afterlife? Is there some way in which they can eat or is there some way they can simulate the experience and sensation of taste or eating?

I definitely obtained contradictory answers to that same question when I reviewed the printed literature as well as the responses of present-day mediums to the same question.

Here are some of the comments from various living mediums and from the literature.

1. I can eat and eat and never gain a pound.

2. We can't eat in the afterlife. Those who enjoyed the physical senses like eating, suffer in the afterlife from withdrawal. In a sense they pay for their gluttony.

3. He still loves eating in the afterlife.

4. We miss eating and sex in the afterlife.

5. Why would anyone ever want to eat?

6. When they come across, they must be weaned from earthly desires such as eating, and are allowed to eat and continue that activity for a little while.

7. They can enjoy the pleasures they enjoyed on earth for a while enjoying what they did with their newly discovered greater powers.

9. They often think about food in the afterlife.

These comments are taken from various books on the topic of conditions in the afterlife and gathered from comments of various living mediums. As you can see, these range from completely contradictory to all of the spectrum in between.

These discrepancies certainly left me confused, so I decided to attempt to address the problem of the discrepant answers given in various books and from various mediums.

In an effort to sort out the varied responses, I asked the medium, Laurie, who is a trusted personal friend, to ask her guides to clarify these issues.

In response to the question of whether or not spirits can retain any predilection for eating in the afterlife the following response was given.

> If eating was important to you in your lifetime, you might save more impressions about eating. It depends on the individual-what was most vivid or important to you in your lifetime. You might want to hold onto a few things.
>
> As you progress up, your memory to recall sensory things goes down, becomes less and less important. There are other things you are able to do that you wouldn't be able to do on the lower levels-other abilities you can have which offset what you may view as a loss of some of your sensory abilities.
>
> One of these is the ability to be in multiple dimensions at one time. It depends on the individual. The more advanced the soul, that soul will know that more things are possible.
>
> If you have a desire, you can travel to another world to experience some of the things you wish, a sort of afterlife vacation.

Asked whether spirits can experience the sensation of eating in the afterlife, Laurie's guides replied:

> With our imagination, memory, and recall, we are able to 'physically' do certain things. The experience is not the same, but very similar. You can tap in and taste through your senses. There are no tongues, but Spirit can sense what a tongue would be sensing. For a short period you do have the ability to eat and continue life as you knew it for a period of time.
>
> Also, a spirit can overshadow a medium or other human being still present on the earth plane, and feel

what they are feeling, taste what they are tasting, and hear what they are thinking. This is a vicarious way that a spirit can also continue to enjoy the senses, such as eating.

Why are there so many different answers from different spirits regarding what life is like on the other side?

My Guide:

Within the framework of eternal truth, there is room for many different individual preferences and convictions.

No two souls would describe love in the same way on earth. When souls come to the other side, there is no one absolute truth. Souls still will retain individual opinions and perspectives, convictions.

Harvey's Guides:

There are no absolutes. What is true for one person may not be true for another. Your experience of the afterlife is what you make it.

Laurie's Guides:

If anything you read does not ring true to you, discard it. There is no one set way. Spirit is always evolving, always changing. That is the wonderfulness of spirit.

Twenty Eight

Divorce

Is divorce always wrong?

My Guide:

It depends on the people. It's not wrong if people are harming each other and can't live in peace. If people are not happy together and cannot solve their issues, they should separate. They should make provisions to fulfill obligations to others, keep contact with others and do the least amount of damage to others involved as possible. They should try to preserve the peace if possible.

Harvey's Guides:

No. A resounding no. Sometimes divorce is a solution for a mistake.

Laurie's Guides:

No. Absolutely not. In regards to marriage, you must learn to pick the right partner and learn to work together, or if you can't work things out, to leave when you are supposed to be leaving, with as little damage as possible.

If by living together you're hurting each other, it is then best if you separate. Many life plans are written with divorce an intention.

Twenty Nine

Encouragement

Can you give some words of encouragement to those in the flesh?

My Guide:

Initiate and formulate your path with confidence, assurance, faith, and trust. Desire to act in goodness and kindness toward and for yourself and others with good intentions and honest endeavor.

Don't worry. That impales you in the moment. It is like quicksand and prevents forward motion by fear.

Strive for attainment, not defeat. Overcome, not succumb. See difficult situations as a challenge, not an impediment and negative people as a lesson, not a persecution.

See things from the vantage point of strength, not weaknesses, triumph, not defeat, accomplishment, not submission.

When you come home, you will understand more, but for now you must see with your inner vision. Be affirmative. Act in love, kindness, and integrity, never doubting that goodness of purpose will find fulfillment and that love will bring the peace you desire. Do not for a minute doubt that you are loved and supported.

You are always being influenced from the advanced spiritual realms with truth and wisdom. Always remember to be a conduit for instruction, encouragement, inspiration, comfort, and truth.

Let the inner wisdom of spirit direct and guide your life. Do not be afraid to ask for guidance. You will never find lasting peace in the world. Let the peace of spirit strengthen you in the difficult situations.

Harvey's Guides:

The best is yet to come

.

Thirty

Exit Points

Do we have exit points in our lives and when do we establish them?

My Guide:

There are exit points we wrote into our lives that we could utilize if we wish. These are written into difficult lives as an option we can exercise.

We know what our exit points are when we come to earth. They are planned at intervals throughout our lives and are set on the other side before we come to earth. We have crisis points or near death situations in our lives. Some of these can be exit points. We write them into our life's plan on the other side as we also write our ultimate death, which may in cases be subject to limited flexibility.

Harvey's Guides:

Yes, we have exit points. There are not one, but many.

Thirty One

Fame

Some books I have read state that titles, fame, distinction, and vanity are no longer important to spirits in the afterlife. Other books I have read depict some spirits as remaining vain and narcissistic in the afterlife. Can spirits still be vain and self-important on the other side? Is fame important in the Afterlife?

My Guide:

People in general realize that all souls are the same, of equal value in the eyesight of God, when they return home. Titles, fame, and distinction are not that important to them. They may be proud of their accomplishments, but they are usually not vainglorious or boastful. The ego drops off.

Those here value service and kindness, unselfishness, more than earthly accomplishments or vanity in worldly attainments.

However, as all souls are not perfect when they come across, if vanity or elevated self-esteem was one of their issues, as might be the case with a prominent person or a star, they may have to work on that facet of their character. If that was their weakness or flaw, it may have to be worked on, as not all imperfections are eradicated by the simple act of death.

Harvey's Guides:

When people come over to the other side, most of the mistakes during their learning experience will preclude narcissism and ego. Some of the channeling equating spirits on the other side to human terms is most likely the author's ego.

Most of the people who arrive from the earth plane have learned some lessons. That doesn't mean that we can't ascend and become better than we were, but most are not as nasty as some people on the earth.

Thirty Two

Food And Sex

Can you explain the discrepancies I found from various books and mediums regarding eating in the afterlife?

Harvey's Guides:

There are no absolutes. Since we retain a vestige of our earth life, we have an opportunity to relive some of the desirable moments. We can actually relive it-no positives will be lost.

Can spirits still have a desire for food or sex in the next life?

My Guide:

Some spirits have no desire for food or sex once they come across. Others have memories of food and sex and still desire both.

If we were particularly enamored of food or sex in our physical lifetime, and we begin to think about food or sex, we can still retain a desire for either. Spirits do not need either one and do not have bodily urges for eating or sexual activity. However, psychological desires for either may persist. We can have sex. Once you lose your bodily urge, it remains only a psychological interest.

If food was important to us in our lifetime some of us have memories of food that are strong. We can still have a wish or desire for food. We don't have hunger or physical bodies to maintain, but if we have a strong psychological desire for something, such as food or sex, we can create the experience or sensation for ourselves.

It is called an illusion because we are not in a physical body but we are able to re-create the feelings realistically and relive the experience in a manner that the perception feels real to us.

We create a vision, experience a sensation or perception that feels real to us. We essentially re-create the experience mentally and it will feel real.

Another time I asked, can we eat or simulate eating in the afterlife?

My Guide:

Yes, we can. However, it is not like we did on earth. We don't have a digestive system or require food.

We create a thought form of a food we liked on earth and create the sensation of taste. We can re-create the experience of eating with our mind and it feels like you're actually eating. It's like eating.

We create things that we valued most on earth. We visualize and sense the food; the taste sensation is real to us.

Harvey's Guides:

Yes. It is possible for them to simulate the sensation of eating - not only for food, but they retain a lot of their earthly pleasures - the earth memory.
As they ascend they need less and less. What they do retain as they ascend is the positives that accrued in their lifetime on the earth. Food is just another basic they brought with them.

If we do choose to eat or have sex on the other side, how is this accomplished without a physical body?

My Guide:

Sex or eating on the other side is not a physical process, but a mentally created experience that we feel.

Thirty Three

Forgiveness

If we planned the situations we encounter on the earth to learn from them, do we forgive others and what are our relationships like on the other side?

My Guide:

Situations are engineered for all parties to learn from them. They are set up for us to learn how to handle difficult situations and make better choices.

Although we planned them to learn from them and realize this on the other side, the feelings we experienced as a result of them are a part of our soul.

We come to realize the harm we did as others do the harm they caused us. We learn to forgive that harm and change ourselves as others do.

We learn to control negative and harmful impulses, both those that affect us negatively such as self-destructive behavior, addictions, promiscuity, as well as those that affect others, infidelity, lies, physical and verbal abuse, acts of anger and exploitation, disregard for the feelings of others.

We learn to control behavior that harms ourselves and others, and to live a spiritually positive life in the flesh, where opportunities to be negative present themselves to us. In this manner we grow as souls.

Harvey's Guides:

Yes, we do discuss things and forgive others. That doesn't mean we choose to be with them. We go our own way.

Thirty Four

Free Will versus Fate

What is fate and do we have fate or free will or a mixture of both when we live our earth lives?

My Guide:

We have free will which is written against the backdrop of pre-planned choices and planned events. We do have the ability to deviate from the planned events if we choose. We are able to change or alter our paths by free will choices. Certain events are likely to happen and are preplanned by us in the afterlife. Those events lead us in a certain direction but we have free choice in our reaction to them and the power to alter the course of our lives.

Things happen to us, circumstances exist, but how we react in and to those circumstances is our choice. What we think, say, and do-our actions-built upon the framework of preset circumstances in which we find ourselves creates the interlocking network of set conditions and variable alternatives.

Harvey's Guides:

Fate is part of our life's path or karma. We can modify it as we go.

Fate is also an excuse for a lot of people.

We have a path but there are lots of mini paths along the way. Our life experiences along the way can modify the direction we're going to. Lots of time fate is interrupted by stumbling blocks we find along the way, and when we come back sometimes we'll take a diversion path.

Even if we have something planned in our life, we have the choice or ability to change it along the way. The path is your life's contract, but it's not set in stone. It's like a highway with an ultimate destination but there are different ways of getting there.

Can we deviate from the path we planned?

My Guide:

We have major events that are set for us to accomplish our purpose, but we are able to deviate from these circumstances if we wish. It is not set in stone, as we have free will and the course of our lives can be altered by decisions we make as we go along.

Harvey's Guides:

When we get to earth, we can diverge from the path we planned. We have free will.

Do we have free will in the afterlife?

My Guide:

We live according to the principles of the spiritual law and abide by these. We cannot lie, cheat, deceive, use, rob, steal, kill, or harm other souls. We have expectations that are there to help us achieve our goals and purposes, but these do not prohibit rest, recreation, or the development of individual interests. These are encouraged. We also have spiritual advisers who help us with our spiritual tasks and their accomplishment.

It is much easier to establish and maintain relationships on the other side because we do not have the limitations of a physical existence such as distance, responsibilities and limited amount of time.

We also have greater awareness of the character of others and therefore of our compatibility or incompatibility with them.

We seek out those with whom we have harmony and affinity. The law of like attraction draws together those of similar mind and heart.

We can sojourn for a brief time with other souls for the purpose of learning or shared mutual interest.

If we love someone very deeply and both souls desire a shared mutual long-lasting companionship, they can blend their paths into a shared common path.

Harvey's Guides:

We have free will on the other side. We can be with someone if we want to and compromise. We can select parallel paths so that we remain together.

Thirty Five

Genetic Ties versus Soul Ties

Since I understand that we reincarnate many times and have had many earth families, are genetic ties or soul ties more important?

My Guide:

We are a group of souls who come together for the purpose of incarnating together to learn lessons. We do have a great respect and gratitude for one another, as we help each other to learn lessons. We have some members who are close and some who are not close. It's like any family, where some members get along better with each other than others.

We have some that are drawn to each other by an affinity in soul and this has no relationship to who we were within a given incarnation. Families on earth are formed for the purpose of learning. We may or may not be close to a particular individual after we transition.

Not all souls are equally close. If there was no deep bond or compatibility on earth, there may be no deep bond or compatibility on the other side. Those of true affection, compatibility, and affinity, are together. We are with those we are compatible with in spirit, whether or not they were a part of our earthly family.

We don't stay with those we don't have a deep bond of love with. We are drawn to those with whom we have the deepest bond of love, whether they were with us in one particular incarnation or not.

We don't need to be together any more than we need to be together on earth. We are free to associate as we please.

Closeness is based on spiritual affinity and love, not on earthly biological ties. We are drawn to those with whom we have a true spiritual love, not necessarily to those we were related to by birth.

Harvey's Guides:

Genetic and soul ties are both important. Genetic ties are important in the sense that spirit is tied to the earth and earth is tied to spirit.

Ties are different here compared with the other side in that you don't have the physical form you have on earth, where relationships are often based on physical attraction.

Physical attraction is not what you would judge other spirits by on the other side. You would judge them by outlook on life and demeanor. Not all spirits are equal.

Thirty Six

God/Source

What is God like and what are God's attributes?

My Guide:

God is the creative and loving divine source of all that is. God is the perfection and purity of all the finest attributes.

God is beauty without ugliness, truth without lies, love without selfishness, peace without conflict, joy without sorrow, goodness without blemish, kindness without malice, the purity and essence of truth, love, beauty, joy, and munificence.

All these things are the attributes of the Spirit we call God. All of us should seek to better ourselves, to pull off the impure attributes, to put on the divinity of God and to let those virtues live within us and be reflected in our behavior toward others.

Harvey's Guides:

God is the best in all of us and present in every spirit, and as we ascend, we become more godlike.

God is perfection. On the earth plane people strive for perfection but can't attain it. On the other side we have the opportunity to cleanse ourselves from our mistakes and transgressions, and become more godly.

Do we meet or see God on the other side?

My Guide:

We don't have a direct encounter with God unless we have a special need for such. We know more because we have knowledge of our own eternal existence. We know how God wants us to grow and learn. We know God's purpose for us and the lessons we need to learn.

We know why we exist and we are given more information as we grow. We know more of God's nature because we know what governs our lives here. We don't know him as a soul but we know of his existence.

My understanding of God is based on the principles we are meant to live by.

I think God is more than just a blind force. God is a directing, purposeful, compassionate, loving, intelligence. Otherwise our environment would have no spiritual laws or guiding principles, and we would have no intended direction.

We don't have to see God personally to know God. We know the truth of God in his wisdom, his principles, promises, and attributes.

When we seek, understand, and incorporate those attributes into us, we know God. And when we act and think in accordance with these tenets, we put on the character of God and are changed.

When we know those attributes, we know God, and when we act in concert with these attributes, we take on or conform to the character, the nature, and persona of God.

When we act in accordance with these precepts we introduce, love, peace, and joy into our lives.

Thirty Seven

Government

Is there government or are their laws governing the spirit world?

My Guide:

The law on the other side is not like the law on the earth. No one is able to commit crime. We cannot hurt each other physically or kill one another. We can't lie, cheat, or deceive. We communicate with our thoughts and our true thoughts and feelings are known. We have no monetary system or need to steal. We have no rape. We have no robbery or extortion. We can't become inebriated or drugged. As such, honesty prevails and we cannot harm one another. We are unable to do it just by the nature of the environment. Those of negative intention desiring to harm one another do not have the opportunity to do so. Also, level of intention separates us. There is a natural draw by vibration to like minded souls.

Harvey's Guides:

Not really. They are not necessary where we are. We learn morality. The afterlife is also a learning experience, and government is not necessary. Negative spirits are segregated away from the upper planes. They can do no harm.

Is there anything we are not permitted to do on the other side?

My Guide:

There are no cheating, no lying, no violence, no harm, no duplicity, no inequities.

There are others in attendance who are given the power to govern, like a benign oligarchy. We don't need a lot of government because we are not able to engage in negative conduct.

We live according to the principles of the spiritual law and abide by these. We cannot lie, cheat, deceive, use, rob, steal, kill, or harm other souls. We have expectations that are there to help us achieve our goals and purposes, but these do not prohibit rest, recreation, or the development of individual interests. These are encouraged. We also have spiritual advisers who help us with our spiritual tasks and their accomplishment.

Harvey's Guides:

> There are some things we can't do on the other side, such as harm others. We can't decide to be a serial killer on earth, but sometimes it happens.

Thirty Eight

Healing/Grief

Besides discussing our recent life with other souls we had relationships with and forgiving each other, what kind of healing is there, structured or otherwise, for souls that have been hurt or injured?

My Guide:

We do have other souls that come to our aid with our troubles and problems. We can ask for help. We have helpers and guides that are very skilled in helping those who have come over injured or ill to recover. We don't need physical help but help with our attitudes, thoughts, and emotions.

We have some who come to our assistance when we were injured or ill. We do have some who need more help than others. It's partly a psychological healing. The light and love and environment help us to heal. We also do have conversations with those we shared our lives with. Some thoughts are energetically healing. We also have energy that is our source of life.

Harvey's Guides:

Most of the healing is acceptance of a new life. The healing will be in the realization that we can ascend. In this life we beat ourselves up for our mistakes. There are frailties on the earth that everyone is subjected to. On the other side we take them as a platform for learning opportunities. Anyone who forgets history is doomed to repeat it. Your spirit has the ability to heal itself. It exists on earth, but we don't have the ability to accept it.

What are some comments you can give me to help those who have lost their loved ones through death?

"Death, where is thy sting, grave where is thy victory (King James Bible, I Corinthians, 15:15-16)?"

When you know that your loved ones are alive, close to you, and awaiting your eventual reunion, the hopelessness of grief can be overcome. It doesn't make the remaining journey through life carefree or easy, but it gives a purpose and a point of focus to help make the steps on the journey a little lighter.

Missing someone you love can be one of the most difficult emotional onslaughts we can face in life. There is no superficial answer or instantaneous cure. But there is a spiritual strength that can make the burden a little lighter-the knowledge that your loved one on the other side is helping you carry that burden with their continued love for you and their spiritual assistance.

When you realize this, you can move forward and accept the difficult challenges of the physical world with a new outlook. Our perceptions create our reality. With that new perception we can create a new life, not without our loved one, for those who truly love one another are never separated. That is only an illusion. Because we can no longer see them with our human eyes or hear them with our human ears, we need to develop our spirit sight and spirit hearing to open the bridge of communication.

We lose the physical but we build hope, patience, and strength, and with that the inner sight of our own eternal existence, and our own loved one's continued existence. With that we can know the unbroken bonds of eternal love and the new communication from mind to mind and heart to heart.`

My guide offered me these words of encouragement when I was undergoing a difficult time of my life.

We stretch ourselves with the demands of the earth. It is the problematic relationships and situations that help us grow and develop the most.

Don't be so influenced by the things you see on television or read, or the dogmatic statements of others, by incorporating those into your life. Do not see yourself by looking through the eyes of others or applying their situations to yourself. Look through your own eyes and do not judge your life by theirs.

When you are unhappy or challenged, state, "This, too, shall pass". It is not a stumbling block, but a stepping stone to greater achievement. Know that the physical doesn't define you. Joy comes from inside. No one can steal the contentment of your soul in eternal joys. Be happy. If you can't be happy because of circumstances, be happy in spite of them. You don't have to be happy with or like the difficult circumstances, but be aware that they are a brief period of challenge and learning, and rejoice in the fact that you have the love of your life here with you every step of the way. Let peace come from that love and contentment from that relationship, from our harmony and from the understanding and wisdom you gain inside, not from the external circumstances.

Joy doesn't always come from the world, but from our inalienable relationship, our abiding love and support for one another from the spiritual union inside, not from the physical circumstances outside. You have overcome those circumstances when you find joy, contentment, and peace inside in spite of them. The outer life is turbulent, unstable, traumatic. The inner life should not be based upon the outer one-we are influenced by it but should not be shaken. The inner strength defeats the outer weakness.

The inner strength is from love, assurance, and spiritual energy, spiritual wisdom. Though all around you quakes and fails, let the inner mind stand in the knowledge of the love of God and the unbroken bond of spirit.

Thirty Nine

Heaven

Can you tell me what heaven is like? Can you tell me the ways in which it is similar to what you expected and the ways in which it is different from what you expected?

My Guide:

I didn't think of it as being a life like ours. I thought of it more as an idyllic place without harm or evil. I expected to see God and to see others who were more angelic than myself.

I didn't know how we would relate with other people or how we would spend our time. I had a lot of questions.

It's nothing like I expected. It is more like an idyllic or nicer earth than a place where exalted beings float around. It's different in some ways from the earth I knew and very much alike in others. We don't have the crime and negative behavior we had on earth. We don't need to maintain bodies or homes, or provide for families.

It's a vista of opportunities, for growth, for learning, and for advancement. It's the beautiful things you wished you had on earth and were never able to achieve.

We do have love and concern and individual relationships that are different with other people as souls. We enjoy things more because they are not tinged with disruption, anger, discord, or destructive behavior. That is not permitted. We can't be negative or domineering or abusive. It is not allowed to inflict harm or abuse one another.

We have personal preferences, choices on our trajectory of development, learning, and recreation. We have closer relationships with some than others. Some we remain with, evolve with, enjoy companionship with, and others we see infrequently or not at all. Some we separate from. We have love for all in the sense that we forgive each other and wish each other well, no harm.

We learn to be stronger, more tolerant, more forgiving both of ourselves and others, and to express love, kindness, and humility. We develop our interests and best assets and share our learning with others. We learn to love unselfishly and practice charity and goodwill.

We occupy ourselves in positive learning experiences. We grow and help others to grow. We live in peace and harmony with all. We develop our talents, interests, and abilities.

All of this is part of what we can do. We can relive parts of our lives we did wrong, and relive experiences we missed. We have opportunities to heal from pain and to heal others.

It is a world both similar to and different from the earth, as we are able to enjoy experiences we missed on earth and to learn and relate with others in improved ways. We work on our flaws and embellish our assets. We create the life we always wanted, which we were not always able to do on earth.

Think about it. No one harms you. You harm no one. You can live the experiences you desired most and missed, all while being a better person, free from harm, conflict, and injury. If that's not heaven, what is?

The happiness and harmony I wished for in "my idea of heaven" are here, but the infinite joy, peace, and happiness are far greater than I expected or ever could conjecture.

It is a world that is more real, more ideal, than the earth ever could be-one in which every good happiness and every non-injurious dream can be realized.

You realize that you are eternal. You realize that you are loved. You realize your life had a purpose. You realize that all the best things you hoped for can come true.

You live in harmony and peace with others-no pain, no insult, no malice, no harm. You have the love and affection and give the love and affection that you always wanted.

Whatever your best and finest hopes were, you realize them. Whatever your most precious dreams were, you have them.

Goodbye to pain. Goodbye to loss. Hello to mastery over faults and flaws. Hello to triumph over injustice and oppression. Goodbye to strife and struggle. Hello to peace and hope. Hello to a place where dreams are realized, and love is complete.

This is my heaven. When you arrive, the script is yours to complete.

Harvey's Guides:

My expectations were few and the experience far exceeded anything I expected. I expected nothingness.

What I found were familiar people- family members that preceded me. I had heard about it but never expected it.

It's different. None of the trials and tribulations that we had on earth are with me. No fighting to get ahead, no worrying about the next paycheck, or keeping people happy.

When I asked them if they thought writing a book would be helpful to those still in the flesh, they answered, It only has to benefit one person. Then it's a success.

It's even a greater learning vista than there was on earth.

Forty

Important to Spirits

What are the things that are important to spirits?

My Guide:

Being with those we love, learning, helping the people we love, reaching the point where we are more free of our former flaws and vices, growing in our understanding and love for others.

We are concerned about freeing ourselves from the wrongs we did and seeking our own development, enjoying love and life and being happy. Peace and comfort and joy are important.

Harvey's Guides:

Knowledge of the mistakes we made in our lifetime, how we can improve, and how we can pass this knowledge on to those who are still alive are important.

Opening in love, sharing love, enjoying the companionship of those we love, are important. Also, learning, working, and helping are important.

Forty One

Individuality

Are we created as individuals or were souls all identical and differentiated by their experiences and lifetimes?

My Guide:

We were all born with individual traits, characteristics, and qualities-with separate identities and purposes, and developed our personalities and values by successive incarnations and relationships.

When we transition to Spirit do we retain individual consciousness and our inherent personality?

My Guide:

We are the same person we were on earth, only a little improved, a little more loving, caring, and kinder.

Harvey's Guides:

We do retain individual consciousness. Otherwise all the learning we have attained on the earth would be for nothing and of no purpose. Even though there are different levels, we have different abilities. However, ego doesn't come into it. Our different talents don't make us better or worse, just different.

Do we retain our individuality when we return to God?

My Guide:

We can become allied with other souls, but we retain some individuality throughout our existence.

Harvey's Guides:

We can always retain our individuality. Otherwise we would lose the knowledge we have gained in our many lifetimes, and our work would have been for nothing. We don't know until we get there, and this is speculation. We like to think so, that we retain personal identity, but we have no personal knowledge.

Are our personalities that we exhibit a true personality that is us or do we put on a fake personality and play a role to learn lessons and teach lessons?

My Guide:

We play a role based upon our choice of family, career, country of origin, and social climate, but in each incarnation our core personality remains the same.

We plan situations to learn from, we do not plan personality.

We have the same personality, interests, characteristics, likes and dislikes when we transition to the afterlife, but we lose the outer housing of appearance, language, gender, and socially acclimatized attributes.

Harvey's Guides:

When they come back to Earth, they only retain personality to carry out the lesson. Personality-there is nothing fake about it.

They don't come back with all the characteristics. They bring back some of the knowledge-negative and positive with them, the negative to avoid, and the positive to reinforce. We're not just playing roles.

Is our personality constant? Does it remain with us when we die or do we have to attempt to recreate it for those we loved who cross over and join us? Are our characteristics retained?

My Guide:

There are certain personal ideas, emotions, preferences, identifying characteristics that separate us as individuals from others. We retain those.

We retain the most important core parts of ourselves. They are not lost. Whether or not we want to retain certain physical characteristics, like how we talked or looked, or cultural habits, depends on us.

The deep feelings and emotions, how we look at life, our type of personality, dominant or passive, jovial or serious, good natured or irascible, is retained, but habits, speech and appearance related to a specific lifetime or experience, are not. Those are irrelevant.

We refine our characteristics and modify our thoughts as a result of the life review. But we gradually improve ourselves. Our main interests, predilections, proclivities, and nature are preserved. We are just working on a new, improved version, hopefully eradicating the flaws over time.

Forty Two

Inspirational Messages

During one particular spirit circle the spirits came through with beautiful, poetic visions.

A daughter of a good friend of mine who had passed early in life presented me with an image of a beautiful leather bound book with gilt-edged pages, and said, "This is the book of our journey and each chapter is one of our many lifetimes. Although we design the plot, the details are not filled in until we live that chapter, and the end has not yet been written. We are composing as we go along."

Another spirit said each one of our souls is unique like a fingerprint. Each individual soul leaves some of his or her fingerprints on the lives of those they touch.

Another soul likened mediumship to a two-way window. The spirits are an inspiration for us, and we are examples for them in the way we live our lives. Both are learning from one another.

Another said your family in spirit is by soul connection not just bloodline.

Another said we visit the world like the waves reaching up onto the shore and then return back out into the ocean of spirit from whence we came.

Another compared mediumship to a jigsaw puzzle. The medium is taking one piece at a time from the spirit and trying to fit it all together into a coherent picture.

One spirit referred to a medium's opening to spirit as a horse who has just had the blinders removed.

Another described his death as being like an eagle flying up into the freedom of the ether.

In the last spirit circle three souls came through with uplifting messages.

One was a professional clown who went by the name of Bumper T. He was a founder of the organization, Caring Clowns of America, a group that reached out to uplift and entertain children who were in the hospital and the elderly in nursing homes. They were a volunteer organization, providing their service free of charge.

Bumper, who was a very caring and charismatic individual, one who loved to entertain, had these comments.

Our spiritual essence manifests itself in all of our acts and deeds. All of these things performed in the material world have their spiritual counterpart.

Try the different chocolates in the box to find out the one you like, the one that fits. Don't be afraid to go out on a limb. Stretch yourself. Nothing is given in vain. When something is done with the right intention, there is never any loss. We each leave our mark on the world in our own special way. You are writing your own autobiography.

Things aren't always as they seem on the outside. Tear the mask off to find the spiritual truth. There is more to life than meets the eye.

Time is like a Chimera. Make the most of it. Do everything you possibly can as you are on the backside looking back at your life before you know it.

Bumper gave an illustration about communication by spirits on the other side with mediums. He likened it to the old radio tower shown on the emblem of RKO pictures many years ago, giving signals out in every direction. Mediums who are attuned and receptive will pick up those signals.

Another spirit guest was a nun, a woman who was self-effacing in her individual character in deference to giving the message.

She said follow your calling. Open your hands and God will fill them. Always have mercy on others. We are all the children of God. Love has many different expressions.

Live an exemplary life. You don't have to be in the church to be of the church. Get the lesson in everything. Something you may consider inconsequential may have a message.

When you are given a pearl of wisdom, it is not just yours to keep, but yours also to give away. Prepare your heart on earth for what you accomplish here will be reflected on the other side. Service, service, service. Go with God.

Another soul mentioned the television character from many years ago, Princess Winter Spring Summer Fall. The Spirit likened this to a paradigm of life where we grow, develop, harvest, reap, and share.

Several other spirits came through referring to the era of Roy Rogers and Hopalong Cassidy. They stated that you don't need to be a star to make your mark on this world. It's not always black-and-white like in the movies. We are all one, and each of us has the hero and villain inside us, and the hero is attempting to defeat the villain. We all have our own battles to overcome. When you live your life right, you are in peace when you're on the other side.

They gave an image of someone shooting an arrow up into the sky and said, aim for the sky. Love wins in the end.

Always try to sing a happy tune. Till we meet again.

Inspirational comments from my guide and myself:

I can't profess wisdom, but I want to impart to others what helped me to overcome.

A true heart, a kind thought is the poetry of God.

Love eternal is the priceless gift celebrated by two souls who love one another.

Love should be a collaboration, not a contest or controversy between one another. It should be a unity, a mutual uplifting and growth.

It is only the ego that says this one accomplishment is greater than that one. All positive heartfelt accomplishments are good.

As the Bible says, you must be broken, not you, but ego, false pride, in order to be a servant of the divine.

Forty Three

Judgment

Is there such a thing as judgment or punishment by God for malefactors?

My Guide:

There is a divine justice which is expressed through karma. We understand the impact of our words and actions on others when we undergo the life review. All things considered, we also gravitate to a level of our own making, delineated by the life we led and the thoughts we had. We select our own destiny and determine our own level by our life choices and intentions.

Laurie's Guides:

You punish yourself because you don't want to be with people with whom you have no affinity, so you gravitate to the lower levels.

In a book called *"Prisoners of Fame,"* by Tanika Palm, the concept of egregores is introduced. Does such a thing exist and what are egregores?

My Guide:

No one I know of has had one. Perhaps others have. I can only speak for myself.

Tanika Palm describes them as thought forms that materialize in the afterlife and are a product of one's negativity.

I was unable to get an answer from my guides or the guides of others in regard to this matter but a book purchased by a mediumistic friend from the Arthur Findlay College of Mediumship describes a similar entity.

The book by Richard Wright describes a channeled experience of Prince Hafed, one of the Magi. The nature of the afterlife depicted in this book is very similar to that described by Anthony Borgia channeling Monsignor Hugh Benson in his books. The afterlife is described as being even better than he had imagined.

In the book, Prince Hafed, looking for Xerxes, couldn't find him. He was told to gaze into a column where he would see a reflection of his own soul and find the Book of Lives or Book of Names in which he could locate or trace the locations of other souls.

King Xerxes had a historical report of being very cruel, power happy, and vain, and harmed many souls at his own expense, for his own gain.

He observed that Xerxes was down in Level One and was permitted to travel down to locate him. Souls in Level Two were described as souls who were living together in their own misery, which was the product of their selfish and inconsiderate lives.

Level One was described as a level in which the inhabitants were isolated, covered by their own self projected force field and were not able to see other souls. They lived in self-imposed pain, and in their own self-imposed prisons, thinking about who they had been and what they had done.

Reportedly, one of his wives who had loved him, as well as several other magnanimous souls, sent love, healing, and positive thought patterns to him and were able to make cracks in the self-imposed prison.

He eventually accepted their love and friendship, which brought him up through the levels to where he currently is now doing service for others in the same manner.

Commenting on this, Laurie's guides state:

You are not judged. You are forced to feel the pain and wretchedness you have imposed on others. The soul creates its own self imposed fetters until it is able to accept responsibility for its actions and become

> more enlightened. The soul must provide love and healing for all those it hurts. In that manner you create your own self-imposed prison.
>
> Some souls on the lower levels appear so distorted that one wouldn't even know that they were human. When you walk past the pillar of truth and see your own reflection you'll see the truth of your character and actions. Some have been horrified to see the true reflection of themselves.

The self imprisonment described in this book sounds very much like the self-created images produced by our negative thoughts referred to by Tanika Palm as egregores.

Forty Four

Karma

What is karma? If people forgive one another and change their hearts, can it be erased?

My Guide:

It's the balance of good and bad. It's like putting money in a bank or withdrawing it. We must balance our account. We are constantly changing our karma by what we say, think, and do. We don't escape it. All of our comments and behavior have results. Those results can be positive or negative. The more positive we put in, the more positive we get out.

It's not so much erasing karma as changing karma. It is first necessary to forgive others and ask for them to forgive you. Change what you have said and done wrong by changing what you do in the future, and you change your karma.

Harvey's Guides:

Karma is not erased because Karma is a lesson and you carry it up through the levels as you ascend. It is necessary to remember karma so we have a vestige of memory and won't repeat our transgressions.

No, you don't have to come back. It's a learning experience. You remember your feelings about a relationship. They do forgive each other.

Laurie's Guides:

You have to ask to forgive each other, and you also need to correct things within yourself. Then you can clear your karma. Otherwise you have to go back for another life and clear that issue.

When souls come across they realize the truth of what they've done. They see the impact of what they've done on themselves and others. You can't progress unless things are changed and done right. You haven't done your work if you can't forgive.

Forty Five

Levels

Are there divisions in the afterlife, different dimensions that souls inhabit based upon their character or level of development?

My Guide:

We have different levels that are much like the strata of life on earth. We are destined to go to a different place based upon our development. We are not able to cross into areas of much higher development. Some are restricted due to the negativity in their lifetime.

If we seek a higher level we can attain it. When we achieve a deeper inner development, a greater discipline, a greater munificence and understanding, a stronger more merciful character, and erase our harmful impulses and behavior, which do harm to ourselves and others, we are able to ascend.

We are at the level that our own inner development places us. We seek greater wisdom, greater rectitude, and admirable character.

We are with those of a similar nature and development. We can be with whom we want. We have choices. Those who have deep mutual love remain with each other. Those who have similar personalities, ways of thinking, and goals, gravitate together. Those who are like-minded congregate. Birds of a feather flock together.

Harvey's Guides:

Everybody enters at a basic level. Different divisions are sorted out later. When you cross over, the biggest problem is assimilating to a new different environment. Life personalities and characters are less of a problem than levels are on earth.

People will ascend to different levels after the basics. Some people will adapt faster than others. It's like taking a test. There are levels. The acceptance of the entry-level determines how far or fast you go.

In one mediumship session, my loved one and guide told me that he was progressing and wanted me to progress, too. I have read books discussing levels or planes of progression in the afterlife, but didn't have a clear concept of what they were. I asked my guide and he explained,

There is progressive development, understanding, achievement, maturation, refinement, or improvement of the soul. Regardless of their station or level of accomplishment, no one soul is inherently better than another. We aren't higher or lower, simply more or less developed.

The levels are progressive in terms of increased understanding or wisdom, a continuum, as in school someone in the seventh grade doesn't abruptly reach eighth grade. It is a gradual learning process, but as we put artificial labels on the stages of learning for distinction, in the spirit world we also apply terminology or labels to identify a stage of progression.

Those in approximate or similar levels of development remain together. They are based on learning and advancement. The levels are separated not by a physical boundary or a geographic context, such as up or down, but by a frequency, a vibrational assignation or spectrum that separates out into dimensions.

The spectrum of light divides out into bandwidths that are continuous but progressive, but also separate, although in a gradation or continuum, into distinct perceivable shades or colors.

So the spirit vibration distributes itself out like the ingredients in a centrifuge, into discrete divisions or segments, strata.

The stratification of the spirit is based upon development of the thought, understanding, and behavior-not just intellectual or academic excellence, but a "moral" or value and character development.

These are levels based upon an individual's conscious understanding of spiritual truth. We do not do what you would call judgment because we are all learning. We do not value one soul more than another. We do define levels of understanding, increasing or decreasing. The person's thoughts determine the behavior. We don't see it as a wall but as a stage of development.

There is a stratification or separation based upon level of progression. It's a grouping of souls of like level of advancement. We are at differing stages and are grouped in that category. We can see more or less advanced levels but are not able to inhabit much greater levels of attainment.

We are in a different vibrational dimension which would correlate with the earth concept of a different space. It's based on learning through trial and error with our learning evidenced in our choices and actions.

What is progression or advancement like on the other side?

My Guide:

Progression is the process of achieving self-awareness, and changing our thoughts, intentions, and behavior through trial and error.

Harvey's Guides:

Passing through the realms involves purification. It is a purification process.

Have you ever been to a higher or lower plane? What is it like?

My Guide:

I've lived through the lower levels as have all spirits on my level. The lower levels have less happiness, peace, less choices.

In regard to the higher levels, we discuss things with those who are from higher levels. I only know of the higher levels through the experience of those who have been there. They say that they are more beautiful than we can imagine. There is more harmony, peace, and selflessness.

Harvey's Guides:

I have advanced through the levels to where I'm at now. They are more or less a training ground. As you pass through, your energy absorbs more information. It is like an infant as it grows, it absorbs a lot of knowledge. I have never visited a higher level.

If there are different levels in the afterlife, is it possible for those who love one another to become separated due to their differing levels of advancement?

My Guide:

For two souls who love one another, they can gauge and regulate their development so that they remain at the same level.

They can deliberately plan and align their mutual development so that they can remain together.

It is also possible for a soul who may be more advanced and loves a soul who is less advanced to remain at the other soul's level and aid them in their progress so that there is no separation.

True love unites and souls can engineer and align their mutual growth to coincide with one another.

Harvey's Guides:

It is unlikely that two souls who love one another would become separated. They can help one another learn and promote mutual development.

Forty Six

Lies

Can spirits lie to one another on the other side?

My Guide:

No, we can't. People will understand by receiving our thoughts whether we are lying or not. A lie detector test is based on the electrical impulses we generate when we are lying. Spirits can automatically decipher the electrical impulse, the intention, the thought of the other soul.

If you were lying to me, I could tell it by reading the thought and feeling you send out. We cannot deceive one another.

We can't lie when our thoughts are known. We don't lie. We can't lie. Our thoughts relay the truth.

Harvey's Guides:

Things are fairly transparent here on the other side. It is not likely that we can lie to one another and get away with it.

Not well. Things are pretty much transparent. Since the trip is purification, lying isn't tolerated. They do regard some behaviors as negative and they are not permitted.

Forty Seven

Life Lessons

What is the purpose of our earth lives?

My Guide:

We don't live on the earth because we need to, but because we choose to. We have more lives than we would have thought. We have so many things we have to learn we need more lifetimes to accomplish them. There is more learning in our Earth lives because there is more turmoil. We learn from our own mistakes and we apply that learning to our future lives.

We can't get through with our lives until we master our needed lessons. We learn as we go along. No one has all knowledge instantly. We are given ideas about how we can approach the lessons we need to learn, but we choose our own method. We are being told what we need to learn, but we have choices among the alternatives.

We each have our individual type of personality and goals. We do have a master plan that is formulated by Source, but we aren't aware of all the details. We are given things as we need to know them.

All we can do is keep working on our faults and weaknesses. No one has a clear or perfect idea of all that is in store for us. No one has all experience they need. We need to keep working as we go along.

We don't understand all things. We don't have awareness of all of our own needs – just what we recognize. We learn from each problem as we go along. We are able to achieve each one separately. Everyone has their own individual goal. We have paths we design. We don't need to learn things until we are ready for them.

People have lives to learn from them, not to be happy from them. We can all be happy to a degree but learning is our major incentive. Some ghosts seem much like they were on earth. They can be angry, bigoted, possessive, and ill-intentioned.

Is there much of a change when spirits cross over into the light?

It depends on the individual. Some people change more than others. We all have different rates of learning, like when we are in school. Most of us learn quite a bit about our behavior, pluses and minuses, when we experience the life review.

When I had my life review, my guide, upon presenting a tour through my life, said, "You weren't evil, didn't wish to intentionally harm others, you were misinformed, misguided, unenlightened – that is, ignorant of the effects of your behavior, "clueless"."

We look at things differently based upon our larger perspective but have the same essential personality. When we become aware of our flaws, we work on correcting them, improving them – polishing them up and putting on the finishing touches.

We work on our personality flaws and consequently our behavior. It doesn't happen overnight. It is a process.

As with all learning, this progresses faster for some and more slowly for others. As our ideas change, so do we.

It is an evolution of character. We all learn ultimately, but our basic personality, that makes us individual, and our better qualities remain.

How do you determine what your life's lesson is?

My Guide:

We feel them. We don't know them. We review our lives and discuss what was most important to us. We decide what our primary focus and challenges were. What was our deepest concern or preoccupation?

> We look at our obligations, works, and most prevalent themes in our lives. Be aware of what most concerns you and is your major issue.

Are we aware of our life's lessons after death?

My Guide:

We are aware of what we were on earth for. We realize what we planned and what our intentions were to learn. We are aware of our purpose and main goals. We are able to see if we achieved them.

We are aware of how much we accomplished and what we failed to accomplish. We see a complete vision- how much we completed of our planned lessons- what we attained and what we didn't. We realize what we need to learn and what we have learned. We see alternatives we could have chosen and project the results of those alternatives. We consider what we should have chosen and make decisions based on our newly acquired knowledge.

We review what we might have done and conjecture what might have been a better choice. We can do an assessment of what we feel we could have done better if we were re-living our life.

What lesson did you learn from your last lifetime?

My Guide:

> I learned to never give up, to keep pressing on in adversity. I learned to make the best of things. I gained strength. I learned responsibility for my actions. I

learned what happens if you fail to set boundaries. I learned that you must make tough choices and follow your heart or you'll lose happiness.

Harvey's Guides:

Humility.

Here are some of the lessons I have learned in my lifetime.

I learned to forgive myself and others, myself because I did things in ignorance, and others because I caused more harm to myself than they did, and if I hope to be forgiven for what I did, it will be easy to forgive them the harm they did.

I learned that knowing to do right is not enough, you must know and then act. You must know right, then do right.

I learned that a world without love is not worth living in.

I learned that you cannot replace someone you love who has died. I would end up with 100 dogs and 1000 men trying to find the one I lost. To be with someone I don't love is not fair to myself or him because I would never be happy when I was thinking of someone else and would never give of myself to him, and that wouldn't be fair to him either. I learned that it is best to wait until you can be with the one you love.

I learned that it is better to be alone than to be with someone who is harming you or abusing you, just to have a companion.

I learned that all the material things in the world, all of the creative pursuits, interests, money, and jobs can never replace loving and being loved.

I learned that you should not permit others to take advantage of you, those who are selfish and care only for their own welfare. You must respect yourself enough to set boundaries.

I learned that if you are unhappy with someone and they are not willing to talk about or correct the situation or compromise, you do not owe it to them to stay there. You deserve happiness too and should leave doing the least amount of harm to others as possible.

I learned that you should not justify doing wrong to others because they have done wrong to you. I thought God rewarded them with money, power, and prestige, so they must be right. But I learned that harming others is not right and the material rewards of the world are not the rewards of God but rewards you have taken yourself. The true rewards are the peace, love, and joy in the spirit, the rewards that no man can steal because he doesn't recognize them and they are treasures you lay up in heaven that moth and rust do not corrupt.

I learned that racial and gender prejudice are very difficult to overcome.

I learned that lying and cheating do not just harm others, but harm you as well. You must not gauge your morality by the immorality of others nor let others' trespasses toward you poison you so that you feel justified in trespassing upon others.

Forty Eight

Life Plans

Is the writing of this book and my mediumship part of my life's plan?

My Guide:

Mediumship and writing were part of your plan but the details are flexible and you can modify them as desired as you go along.

You were meant to find me, change your life, and we were meant to progress together.

Harvey's Guides:

The questions will be given to you when the time comes. Nothing will be lost. You were meant to do this work. It was passed down from your heritage. Your grandmother wasn't the first. She brought the genetics down with her from earlier lives.

You will influence other souls that will eventually be reincarnated.

When we pass, it's a new beginning. This is not the end. Everyone we bring along with us on earth, they extend our life after our death. We influence everyone we come in contact with. We change their life.

For people who don't have children, it is not the end. They influence others.

It is very likely you will return with this gift at a very early age, rather than later in life.

Forty Nine

Life Review

Is there a life review on the other side and what is it like?

My Guide:

Yes. We do have a life review. It's learning. We can't learn without seeing ourselves, both good and bad. It can be quite humiliating and humbling. We feel the pain that our words and actions have caused others.

Truth is like a spotlight that shines on all things and illuminates them. We see ourselves objectively. We see ourselves from the viewpoints of others. People have their own opinions, but once they see themselves from others' eyes, they do modify their opinions.

Some may not progress as quickly as others. It involves a willingness to see objectively, and a willingness to change. Most souls want to progress. But some progress more quickly than others.

This involves not only a change of thoughts, but a change of actions. The change of thoughts must be demonstrated in a change of behavior. Coming to earth and changing our previous behavior determines whether we've internalized our learning and have changed based upon our past mistakes.

Harvey's Guides:

Yes. There is a life review on the other side. It is not a negative experience.

Fifty

Light Anomalies

What are the light forms or anomalies that some people have captured by camera in cases of active hauntings?

My Guide:

We are energy. Both human and non-human energy can manifest in different forms.

Laurie's Guides:

These are most often other dimensional beings. By moving objects or causing anomalies, it doesn't necessarily mean that they are negative. Often, they are trying to communicate with you, and they are a group of beings that don't have language.

For instance, Silver is a much more evolved energy being that has acquired the ability to connect with the language. They communicate nonhuman energy experiences.

Fifty One

Loss

Are there any comments you can make that will help those who have suffered loss?

My Guide:

> The physical cannot be relied on and will always let you down. In spirit there is no loss. Trust spirit.

Fifty Two

Love

There is a quotation I would like to include from Mavis Pittilla's book, "*Mavis – With Spirit*", (54). She is talking about a couple who lost their son in a tragic automobile accident. She states, "So you see that spiritual contact set them on a road of service, and I think it was very sad but true when my friend said, 'I had to lose the greatest love of my life, to find the pathway to God.'" I cannot help but cry when I read that, because I recognize, that's me. Through his loss, my loved one has given me the greatest changes in me, my soul, that I have ever undergone. He has turned me around completely, and now we are on a path, a journey of learning and seeking together. I do not recall where I read this, but the comment was, "In seeking the spirits of those they loved, many have found their own souls."

What is love in your opinion?

My Guide:

> Placing one's welfare above your own. Sharing. Companionship. Devotion. Openness and mutual happiness and peace. The joy of companionship.

Harvey's Guides:

Love is sacrifice, willing to sacrifice everything for another.

How would you describe love?

My Guide:

It is the environment that we are in that leads us to desire to help, to progress, to serve, to play a part in the healing and teaching, the forward movement of all souls. The love is the ability to appreciate, empathize, and have compassion for all souls. It is the God spirit within us that has concern and kindness, caring for all souls' welfare and development.

We also have a love that is more personal, a love between souls that is more intense, a bond that is closer, an intimacy and devotion that is more ardent. Some have a love that is built on deep inner compatibility, respect, and affinity, a closer tie, a deeper love, an indissoluble bond. These are mated or bonded or united in spirit. Those are souls with a stronger love and deeper dedication to one another.

There is an intense personal love between individuals.

There is a regard for the welfare of all souls.

We are the ambassadors of love from spirit for the world.

Love is the same, but it inhabits different roles. The love of helping, as we help children to grow and develop, the love of friends, as we support and enjoy each other's company as our paths cross, the love of humanity as we seek to improve conditions and interpersonal relationships, and the love of companionship, of support, of partnership in sharing with someone with whom our paths have merged and blended, with whom we share a common path or where our paths are united.

On the other side, we also have a greater understanding of unconditional love, a love beyond all words and all limits.

I always read about how important it is to be unselfish in order to progress in the afterlife. Is it wrong to want love or a companion for yourself?

My Guide:

It's selfish if you only care about yourself. If you care about yourself and others, it's not selfish. We cannot be completely in denial of or oblivious to self as long as we are an individual, but the degree to which we are able to set aside our own interests in the concern for the welfare of others determines how unselfish or less ego-based we are.

This does not mean it is desirable to completely efface our own welfare or needs, or to let others take advantage of us, but merely that we are to consider the effects of our actions on others, and to treat others with love, respect, and concern, as we wish for ourselves to be treated.

We are to promote both our own welfare and happiness and the welfare and happiness of others, to treat others as we wish to be treated, to balance between our own fulfillment and happiness and that of others, to be able to receive love, give love, love and honor ourselves and others.

Harvey's Guides:

Selfishness is when you don't share and that includes your emotions.

People frequently want love and companionship, especially initially in the lower realms. As you ascend, it becomes less and less important. What is important is to purify your thoughts and actions. As we ascend we get more godlike and less selfish. That part of your personal being which requires personal love is less important.

However, that may not be true for everybody. There are no absolutes on either side.

Some of us may ascend to a place we want to stay at. It's possible to remain in your own Eden or Utopia. God won't tell you that you have to leave that.

Can we stay around people we love and have affinity with in the afterlife?

My Guide:

That's what they mean by the law of attraction. We attract those that are like us, those with a common bond and perspective. We all have those we are closer to. We stay with those for whom we have the greatest affection and with whom we have the deepest bond.

Harvey's Guides:

Yes. We do stay around people we love and have affinity with. This becomes less important as you advance to higher levels.

Can you say a few things about the compatibility between two people?

My Guide:

We all have our own vision and our own direction. We have values that we embrace. When two people are aligned in their thinking, they are happy.

When they have similar emotional, physical, spiritual, and intellectual viewpoints, or character, they are compatible.

These shared qualities produce unity, companionship, compatibility, and bonding. These produce harmony, contentment, peace, joy, fulfillment, and a thriving relationship in which two partners have entered a path together to shape their mutual future growth, accomplishments, happiness, and unity.

Harvey's Guides:

As on Earth, some have shared or common interests, goals, and preferences.

Robert Brown, the medium, states, "True love cannot be faked."

Raymond, Sir Oliver Lodge's son, conveys this message from the afterlife. "You gravitate here to the ones you're fond of (*Raymond, or Life and Death*, 229). I have learned over here that everyone is not for you. If not in affinity, let them go, and be with those you do like (232).

What is the essence of the spiritual bond of companionship, of pairing?

Although we retain our individual identities we become one in our love, one in our mutual support, one in our concerns, one in our efforts and mutual endeavors, one in our future shared growth, and one in our commitment to one another.

The best thing we can have in this world is genuine love. When money fails, when jobs fail, when health fails, true love will never fail. It is the one thing we take with us from this life. All other things may be convenient, but are in themselves unfulfilling.

All of these without love are empty, are vain, are evanescent. They are all temporary vanities that are needful to an extent in this life for sustaining the physical, but are as nothing without the inner sustenance of love.

Fifty Three

Mediumship

One of the facets of mediumship that I have been personally working on is how to tell whether something I hear is from Spirit or from myself. That is, I wish to refine my ability to remove self from the readings or information I get, and become a clearer channel.

I recently attended a class given by an excellent medium in southern California. This was a development class with many various engaging exercises.

One of those that I found to be particularly useful was a remote viewing session that we as a class took part in. For those who may not be familiar with remote viewing, this is an ability that some individuals have and can develop to be able to see the characteristics and appearance of, and to obtain information about a remote location or event.

Remote viewers have been employed by the government in sensitive political situations or issues. They are also used by some police departments to attempt to locate missing people, or victims of crime.

Although I do not regard myself as a developed remote viewer, the exercise was very interesting as far as helping me in my mediumship work. The class was given the assignment with a handout asking numerous questions that identify a situation or place, such as was it a place of nature, a man-made structure, or a combination. Other questions concerned colors, smells, sights, and activities apprehended.

The medium made a video of herself engaged in this activity, and we were given the task of identifying the activity and surroundings as best we could following a meditation.

What I learned from the exercise was how to better discern information that is given to me from spirit and information coming from my own mind. I found after reviewing the results that there were certain phrases or images that popped into my mind that were totally unrelated to anything I was thinking about. Others were things that my own mind concocted or impressions that I myself, created.

In other words, I learned how it felt to tell the difference between something that is being given me and something that I, myself, have engendered.

This type of distinction is important in helping the medium to disengage their own thoughts and interests, their own convictions and beliefs, and to become a passive, clearer channel for information.

It was a very important take-home lesson, one which I can use in the future, to be able to tell what I am thinking or improvising, as opposed to what spirit is trying to give me.

At a recent spirit circle I was re-introduced to the importance of "giving what you get" rather than interpreting.

One sitter gave me an image of lions. They were two golden lions' heads and I said, "What is your connection with lions?" The sitter said, "Oh, my God. I can't believe you just said that. My father was a huge participant in the Lions Club. It was a huge part of his life".

I had the good discretion to say exactly what I got. My logical mind and previous frame of reference immediately thought of the MGM lion and the Lion King movie. But it goes to show that was my analytical mind taking over and if I had said that instead, the sitter wouldn't have recognized the symbol that the Spirit gave.

How does communication work?

My Guide:

It's all about the energy. As your grandmother's childhood friend, Charlotte, said, it's so difficult to come back. It takes so much energy that only a few spirits can keep up a prolonged conversation. If we have the privilege of guiding someone, and notice I said privilege, we are given, endowed with more energy to aid in the communication. Guides who converse with mediums, in particular, are given more help, greater energy and practice at opening the energy channel or force field.

We are energy and we are learning to control and use the energy, to manipulate it with our will and thoughts. A strong positive emotion such as love bridges the gap. It opens communication with us with a powerful emotion. Like a gravitational field, it affects the energy of objects around it. We can transmit our thoughts and images with a harnessing and beaming of our energy.

As light and sound are carried on waves in the physical world, so the higher vibrations of Spirit thought can be transmitted directly from spirit to spirit.

What factors enhance communication?

My Guide:

You have two factors that are important in enabling you to connect with the realm of spirit. The first is the direct contact of the soul with love. When you feel love toward another soul you will be able to reach them. We have a connection with those we love.

We are united in the sense that there is a bond of love that keeps us in touch. We are not only in touch, but we are with that person even though we are not recognized in ways that are conventional in the physical world. That is the most important factor in establishing a connection with a person who has passed.

We also have another important consideration. We need to make our vibrations closer to those in the spirit world. One way to raise our vibration is to become a more spiritual person. Be more aware of spirit and more attuned to spirit. You need to keep your vibrations more elevated. Be more positive, lifting up your heart with love and joy. Become uplifted by these. Seek these faculties. Be truthful, loving, kind, caring, and unselfish.

These will make you more gifted in spirit. Use your intentions for loving contact. We will hear you and help you. Draw closer to us and we will be closer to you. Be more sensitive, honest, and sincere, more empathetic, and loving. Don't be afraid to give of yourself and to trust.

We are waiting for you. We are able to reach you. We will help and guide you. We are able to help you grow. There are things that you can seek. We are able to maintain the bond of love across the chasm of death. For there is no absolute death, only a change.

Sometimes I can't tell whether words in my mind are mine or yours. How can spirits on the other side tell which

thoughts are their own and which thoughts are being sent to them from another spirit?

My Guide:

We can tell because we don't have the same barriers and encumbrances that we have on earth. We know that the thought we are receiving from another spirit is not our own thought.

We are able to decipher its origin. We are aware of who it is coming from. We can tell that it is an energy apart from our own. Your perception is clouded by your fleshly sheath.

When you come across, your perception will be clear. When you are on the earth you can tell whether another voice directed toward you in speech is from someone else or from yourself. In the same manner, someone's energetic thought directed at us in the afterlife can be perceived as coming from that soul and not from ourselves.

Can channelers improve their accuracy?

Laurie's Guides:

The clarity of the channel is of paramount importance in the accurate transmission of message from spirit. What the medium thinks or the medium's strong opinions can influence or color the message.

Why do some mediums who demonstrate true ability not always reflect spirituality or ethics in their personal lives?

You would think, since mediums are in touch with the spiritual world, that they would be highly spiritual or evolved beings. I have found that this is not necessarily the case.

Mediums, as they are human, are subject to the same flaws as the rest of us. I have seen purported mediums who are highly financially motivated and materialistic, others who are highly opinionated and fixed in their beliefs, some have anger problems and can be very crude, as well as others who are petty, selfish, and jealous.

Because we have agreed to serve in the capacity of being a link or channel with the world of spirit does not mean that we don't have human flaws as well. As in any echelon of society, mediums can be more spiritually evolved or less spiritually evolved, more or less beset with the human flaws of jealousy, envy, domineering spirit, inflexibility, lack of charitable behavior, as are the rest of us.

As with any human being, although we may admire or look up to their achievements, this is not necessarily correlated with their spiritual level of development.

Mediumship –Team Spirit

There is another feature that helps us grow as mediums. This is the ability to tap into a spirit connection that someone else in the circle has established.

It is an ability that can be intended and developed. When we set our intention to do this it was amazing to see how many of the mediums in development Circle were able to connect with the energy of the same spirit, and each one of us got a different detail about their personality or life.

It may have been that the spirit chose to give a certain detail or fact to a certain medium, or it may have been something specific about each medium's knowledge base, experience, or personality that made it easier for the Spirit to convey that particular piece of information to them.

I have learned that 3 to 12 mediums working in harmony and each contributing pieces of information can be better than just one. Each medium brings a different set of experiences and knowledge base to the reading, and they have unique personalities and perspectives that give Spirit a diversity of avenues through which to deliver their message. Each one of us has our own unique talent. I enjoy working as a team. This also gives each one of us a chance to relax and get the message with less pressure.

Fifty Four

Negative Souls/ Entities/Ghosts

People who have led miserable, extremely selfish and destructive lives and mistreated other people on earth, how is their reception initially on the other side? Is all forgiven or is there a period of adjustment?

My Guide:

They are usually very surprised at the love that awaits them. They are ushered in as gently as possible. They create their own form of purgatory in their unwillingness to change. If they are open to change, they will be helped.

They are aware of the pain and damage they have caused other people, and, in order to progress, must themselves remedy the insults. They are not able to progress without adjusting their attitudes and softening their hearts.

We are able to achieve different levels based on the state of our spiritual development. When you have a very big difference in the moral/ethical development, there is a separation between those who are malicious and others who are more elevated in character/development. Progress is open to all, but must be desired within the individual.

There is an adjustment for those who practice evil and inflict intentional harm on others. Progress may be slow or rapid based upon the individual will and capacity for enlightenment, but there are those who will aid or assist the individual soul in its progress, but progress cannot be imposed, and must be initiated from within.

There is a larger adjustment for those of undeveloped character and of intentionally spiteful behavior.

Harvey's Guides:

They have to stay in the lower realms and review all the harm that they have caused and experience all the pain before they can ascend.

Are there any souls that never progress because they are too negative or choose not to learn?

My Guide:

As there are some who are unwilling to change on earth, there are those who are unwilling to change in the spirit world. Progression entails an act of will, and does not occur spontaneously and uninvited.

If someone has no desire to progress they will not. There are so many levels of people here. Some advance fast, some slow, and some not at all.

If it is their will to do so, they can remain at the lower, more negative levels indefinitely. No one is forced to change-only invited, sometimes persuaded, but it always must be a free will agreement by the individual soul to change and to embrace change.

Harvey's Guides:

Yes. The opportunity is always there to progress, but they may choose to stay and relive their conquests, their high points- personal achievements at someone else's expense.

Some choose not to progress because of that. They have to feel superior and they feel that anything else is a weakness. To progress you have to surrender to get to a higher place. They have to do that. There are some souls that choose not to progress indefinitely.

Can negative spirits or other circumstances intimidate people who have died and cause them to stay on earth rather than cross over?

My Guide:

They cannot be prevented from crossing over, but they can be intimidated to the point that they feel they cannot cross over.

We have some on earth who are intimidated, fearful, confused, or simply don't want to cross over. Some can be negatively influenced by a dominating negative spirit. Others may feel ties to an earthly location or person, or seek justice or vengeance. We have souls who help those who wish to cross over. Both souls who are in Spirit or physical can assist.

Harvey's Guides:

I think it's possible, but there are actually people on earth that can break that bond and help them cross over with a love connection. The same way we tell someone in dire straits on earth, it's okay to move on. Some of these souls are slightly confused.

No one can keep someone from crossing over. Their earth fears might still be with them.

Can negative spirits affect people on earth or possess them?

My Guide:

Yes. People who are in a weakened state or susceptible state-those who are unstable, those who choose negative or invite them in, those who are under the influence of drugs, are more at risk. People can be and are influenced by negative spirits and can be controlled or possessed; in other words, directed by the more powerful spirit.

Harvey's Guides:

Yes. There are strong negative spirits that can affect us on earth. But they have no power to harm those on the other side.

The impetus to do the right thing can be all powerful and allow for a smooth transition on the other side. People that are tested here and succeed usually ascend quickly.

Yes, they can be affected by negative spirits on the other side. We call them mentally ill, such as serial killers. Some people can be possessed.

Fifty Five

Negative Levels

Are there less developed realms or vibrational levels in the afterlife?

My Guide:

There are so many different things here that are unlike what we have on earth. Some realms are the habitation of souls that are not as developed, and they desire to engage in harmful behavior.

Not only human, but negative souls that have never had a human life are in existence. There are forces and entities that are negative by choice. These are not all human. They can influence and interact with humans. They have been called the demons. They are souls that intend harm. Some are non--human.

What are the negative levels like in the afterlife?

My Guide:

They are the worst of all places. If you were to take all the good from the earth and live only among the spiteful, the liars, the cheaters, the thieves, the peace breakers, the deceivers, the opportunists, the violent and the criminals, the murderers, you would have their environment. To live subject to those who are malicious like you is hell. They torment one another and live in darkness and despair.

Harvey's Guides:

They make their own hell. They try to replicate what they did on earth. They try to reenact their conquests at others' expense.

On the other hand, people that exercise free will and turn down temptation quickly ascend. Temptation is a fact of everyday life. What we do about it makes a difference. Resisting temptation on the earth plane, comes with many rewards, which are mostly non-monetary. Others will look up to you as an example.

That's the ultimate reward on earth. Do good. Don't ask for any reward. They'll come anyway.

Fifty Six

Negativity

Do you have anything negative on the other side?

My Guide:

Here we have much more protection and direction than we did on earth. Many negative things were permitted to occur on earth.

On earth, negative human and non-human spirits can do harmful things to people.

What is the repercussion of negative thoughts in the spirit world? Are they permitted? What effect do they have on ourselves and others?

My Guide:

They have a more distinct and direct effect than they have on earth. They do affect the people who are the recipients, as well as ourselves. They are not a very good thing. They make an impression on us in the sense that they darken our spirit, they lower our vibrations.

We need to practice on how not to be affected by negative or annoying situations-to get out of them on earth or to live with them, looking above and beyond them, to the best extent possible-not letting them define us or entrap us in an endless cycle of negativity.

On the other side we don't need to worry as much. We are confronted by the truth in any situation with another soul, and each is forced to see his own flaws, faults, negativity, and the effects of his actions on others. In that way we work to correct our negative thoughts and actions. We cannot exist in a positive, elevated environment with negative thoughts, and all parties concerned must eradicate them.

Fifty Seven

Overlay of Feelings

How do spirits impress their feelings upon people?

My Guide:

They can make you feel like they feel. They project their moods outward and impress them much like we as humans project our feelings through our behavior and speech. They direct their energy to manipulate people's moods. It is a control of energy to affect people physically or mentally.

In spirit we can hear the thought and feel the feeling directly rather than interpreting it from words or behavior.

Harvey's Guides:

By getting them out of their comfort zone. Most people are not comfortable with spirits. It happens by telepathy. Even though in the physical we have bodies, we still have spirits. All of us have things we can recall in our memory. Spirits can recall these feelings in us.

I was given an example of how spirit can overlay a thought or feeling on us at a recent Spirit circle. All of a sudden in the midst of delivering messages I got the most beautiful feeling of happiness and love for all.

It was overwhelming and breathtaking, and I wanted to get up and shout. It was my guide and the spirits impressing that feeling on me.

I recognized as spirits we can do that on one another. The difference is that on the other side we would know that feeling was not "ours," or originated by us, but came from "outside," from someone else.

That is why in hauntings where some people experience mood or personality changes they don't realize they are coming from Spirit or Ghosts or have been residual feelings impressed upon and stored by the environment. They don't realize this or know how to control those feelings because they are absorbing them from outside and are unaware of it.

Fifty Eight

Oversoul

Is there an oversoul and what is it? Does only a part of our soul incarnate and we leave a part in the afterlife?

My Guide:

The oversoul is the greater awareness, the composite knowledge from all of your lifetimes.
We have a second part of ourselves that we don't use on the earth. We don't have all of our soul with us when we come down. It is like a memory bank of our previous incarnations and we access this knowledge and blend our souls with it when we return.

You are still the same person but you're rejoining memories of the rest of your existence.

It just happens automatically when we come back. We re-blend with the other parts of our existence.

When you are on the earth, it's like you have a part of your life when you are home, another in your career, another part in a marriage, another part single, different parts in different places with different activities. You're the same person living different experiences and growing. We learn and change but our core permanently remains the same.

What you refer to as the oversoul is not a separate soul. We have a part of our energy that remains here as a record of our experiences. It is just a larger part of ourselves like a memory bank. It's like the cloud-the rest of the data we're not using. We don't need to reunite with it when we come back. We are the oversoul. We just become aware of the rest of ourselves.

Harvey's Guides:

There is a part of us that stays in the afterlife when we reincarnate. It is an imprint of our energy, like a photocopy or a recording- there to be addressed when needed. It has the imprint of our prior lives. Those in the lower realms may not have the ability to access it.

Laurie's Guides:

We are just a fragment-no more than 15% of the oversoul. The oversoul can change with the experiences it accumulates, but you are the sum total of all your experiences and you will always be you. We retain the same individual personality and consciousness, slowly evolving on the basis of our cumulative experiences. As you continue to exist through all the levels, you will always be you.

If you choose to reunite with source, you will be an individual formless spark within the greater energy of the divine.

Spirit is more as opposed to less.

This answer was given when I asked about how much we can experience in the spirit world as opposed to the physical.

Fifty Nine

Past Lives/Memories

Are we automatically aware of our past lives when we die?

My Guide:

We are aware that we have had prior lives but we aren't aware of what they were like. We learn what they were like if we look into it. We ask our guide or consult the Akashic records. We can just become aware of it or we can re-experience parts of it or feel it if we want. I could draw upon my memories of them when I came across. I did have awareness of them.

We become more aware of the lives we've had before than we were on earth. We don't recall every detail. I just know some. We can't store it all so easily, but we can reference it.

We know some of them, but we don't have every detail at our disposal. We know about them. It's like having a summary of our past performance. Recalling all the details is not important. We can access the record of that life of our soul if we want to obtain more information.

I do recall most of my life on earth but may not remember some small details. I don't think you would either. But some things are very important to us, and we do remember them.

Harvey's guides:

Barely. We have fleeting memories- not a lot of detail. It is similar to the déjà vu we have on the earth plane. As we ascend, these memories become part of our spirit.
Depending on how far we ascend, they are less and less of the total.

We do not necessarily know that other souls were in a past life with us. It is a possibility but not a necessity that we know that they were in a past life with us.

I do not think we automatically know about our past lives. We retain a vestige of our last one. As we go higher, more information becomes available to us.

Has my guide ever had other human incarnations with me before and has Harvey's guides ever had a human incarnation with him?

My Guide:

We have had many lives together.

Harvey's Guides:

Yes.

What is the real me relative to my multiple past life personalities?

I have read some books in which the authors have described past lives in the sense that we are multiple separate identities or that our past incarnative selves are different or separate parts of us. It is as though we are fragmented personalities and somehow they are separate and different from us even though we were them at one time. This explanation was difficult for me to understand in the sense that if I had a past life that person is somehow separate from me, and that I am really multiple personalities. Somehow, that reminded me of the multiple personality disorder I studied as a student in my psychology class. I asked my guide for help. He explained in this way.

> We are each one soul, but our previously incarnated selves are various steps in the progression of that soul, various "identities" or presentations of the same soul, based upon the circumstances and environment of a given life. Our past incarnated selves are not separate souls, but separate manifestations of the one soul, separate characters or roles we played, but it's always us doing the playing.
>
> For example, we are the same soul as when we were young, but may have had different ideas or behavior along the maturation process. We weren't different people per se, but one person growing and evolving with progressive experience. In the present we are the

sum total of all we have been previously, or the product of our prior knowledge and experiences.

We can enter into a past life and relive moments of it. It's like viewing a movie and then entering into a character and being a part of the movie. Take your own youth, for example. You are not quite the same individual you were when you were young because you have learned from experiences and you think differently. Through your memory you can go back and act like the person you were, think like you thought, feel like you felt. You can enter into and be that person again temporarily if you wish. So it is with past lives. That person was you and you can put on that character as you would a garment for a while if you wish.

I have read some authors who claim that we are instantly healed of all our pain and trauma when we cross over to the other side. However, I have also seen accounts of reincarnation which indicate that we can carry trauma and fears from our past lives into another lifetime, which would indicate that we do not heal completely. Which is the case?

My Guide:

We have memories in our soul and even if we are healed of the pain, if those memories are awakened, we can re-experience the feelings associated with them. Other events can remind us of them and we re-experience the emotions associated with a similar personal event.

Even if we are healed of them and they are no longer a conscious concern or preoccupation, the memory of them is never erased. We can carry that memory into future lives and re-experience it in its effects.

The lessons are an indelible part of our soul, and when we learn them we can break the repetitive cycle of unproductive behavior. Without some memory of that effect of their consequences, we would not overcome that behavior.

Harvey's Guides:

Remembering the fear, pain, and suffering, no matter how thin the vestige of memory is, can help us avoid the same pitfalls in our present life.

Yes, we can carry through and remember traumatic events. It's no different from déjà vu. Most people have experienced it more than once.

If we forgive one another the injuries we did to each other when we convene on the other side, why is it that some people are negatively affected in a current life by unhappy past life experiences that they seem to not have gotten over?

My Guide:

When we return to the other side and see the reason for our lives, the lessons to be learned, and evaluate our behavior one toward another, we forgive one another, but the feelings we had remain a part of the fabric of our character, so that we do not make the same mistakes in the future, avoid the negative situations, or cope with them better.

Otherwise, we wouldn't learn from our mistakes if we didn't feel their effect. Although we do not bear grudges and learn to coexist harmoniously, to relate to one another or interact peacefully, it does not mean we have to or want to spend much time with that person. If we are different or not drawn together by similarity of interest, goals, or personality, we separate and react in peace when we encounter them again.

Harvey's guides:

We must retain knowledge of our past mistakes or we would repeat them again.

Sixty

Personality versus Roles

When we come to the earth, does the individual we are reflect our true personality or are we someone different in the afterlife who puts on a fake personality and is playing a role to learn lessons and teach lessons?

My Guide:

We are the one personality who is truly us, colored by the gender we have taken on and the culture we inhabit. We are not just playing a role. We are living through and responding to the situations we have set up for ourselves to learn from.

We play a role based upon our choice of family, career, country of origin, and social climate, but in each incarnation our core personality remains the same.

We plan situations to learn from, we do not plan personality.

We have the same personality, interests, characteristics, likes and dislikes when we transition to the afterlife, but we lose the outer housing of appearance, language, gender, and socially acclimatized attributes.

Harvey's Guides:

We are not just playing a role. We are the person or energy in the bodily form we inhabit. We are living out the scenarios we planned for ourselves. But we are the whole being, not just the outer form. Otherwise we wouldn't learn from our mistakes.

When they come back to Earth, they only retain personality to carry out the lesson. Personality-there is nothing fake about it.

They don't come back with all the characteristics. They bring back some of the knowledge-negative and positive with them, the negative to avoid, and the positive to reinforce. We're not just playing roles.

Sixty One

Pets

Do pets reincarnate?

My Guide:

They do reincarnate and progress as we do. They are here for service. They are a source of solace and aid for human beings.

Harvey's guides:

Pets have had multiple lifetimes on the earth like we have.

How can spirits communicate with animals on the other side?

My Guide:

It's a universal thought language. No words are necessary. We automatically impart understanding. The thought itself, a remembrance of an action, an intention, a feeling, an image, can all be imparted from mind to mind, from soul to soul, regardless of species, or language barriers. We are able to communicate more thoroughly and accurately without misunderstanding.

Spirits communicate with each other on the other side through thought transference. They can also use ordinary language or words in their thoughts if they wish.

Harvey's guides:

The same way we communicate with spirits-by thought and emotion-especially if there is a love bond. They can understand what makes us happy as we can understand what makes them happy.

Can animals reincarnate and evolve and become human?

My Guide:

No, they don't. They are a different class of creation. We are souls of a particular type along a spectrum and keep our own individuality within our division. We retain the classifications we were created with, but we all do have the power to evolve within our category.

Harvey's guides:

In the afterlife, everything has a chance to get higher and higher, and since we are greeted by our pets, I think they would possibly go with us and evolve into human form.

Sixty Two

Physical Phenomena/ Movement

I have witnessed physical phenomena a number of times. I was touched once very firmly on the upper arm. I was so surprised I turned my head to look at my arm and my skin was being depressed and moved just exactly as if someone physical were touching it. This was on my birthday four years ago. It occurred at a moment I was very distraught and was talking to a loved one in spirit who was comforting and reassuring me.

Another instance of spirit affecting my physical surroundings occurred when I was again speaking to my loved one in spirit. The seat belt alarm suddenly went off where no one physical was sitting in the seat. I was alone in the car and it was a bucket seat. My loved one was responding to something I was thinking that was very intense.

In a similar manner, while I was thinking of my loved one while I was working on the computer, I had very strong emotions. At that exact moment the computer started to give the loudest feedback I have ever heard for no physical reason at all. It has never done that before or since. My loved one was affirming that he was there and getting a message across to me.

Several times when I have been on the phone with a friend of mine in the medical field who is also a physical medium, some very unusual static has come over the phone line. On one of those occasions my friend was telling me something private and had just said, maybe I shouldn't be telling you this but I will. Just at that moment spirit intervened and some very peculiar static came over the phone line for about 25 seconds. We both ended up laughing over that one.

I have also seen a compass needle deflected in intelligent response to questions for spirit in her presence.

Several times my loved one in spirit has made lights that were off go on and lights that were on go off, each time in an intelligent response to something that was happening or something we had been talking about. My loved one has a great sense of humor and one time I was lying in bed in the dark at night and I asked him (thinking about a house on the other side) what does our home look like? And instantaneously he turned the lights on in the room, which made perfect sense, because for all practical purposes, he is living with me. Another time I was jotting down some notes on paper and struggling in the dark because I was too lazy to get up and turn the lights on. At that exact moment my loved one did it for me.

As I mentioned in my first book, while I was at a development seminar in the Bahamas with a group of mediums, I saw an ordinary table that we brought in spontaneously off the patio of our meeting room that was not rigged, move across the floor, turning as it went, under its own power. I wouldn't have believed it if I hadn't seen it myself. I have no doubts it was under spirit power as it happened in broad daylight in an ordinary room with my friends and I in no position where we could have propelled it.

Here are some other questions I have asked spirit about physical phenomena.

One of the signs of spirit or ghostly activity documented on many of the popular ghost shows on television is the movement of physical objects by spirits. A phenomenon purportedly performed by some spirits at physical séances is apport of objects. When spirits move objects does it occur by force or apport?

My Guide:

> When people see or document things moving, it is commonly by energetic force, not apport. We can control our energy to move or lift things in the physical world. When we move things we are able to let people know we are present.
>
> Apport can occur; it is not impossible. We have the ability to create or dissolve objects in our world. It is more difficult in the physical. It is not impossible to materialize ourselves to be seen, or to materialize other objects. We are using our energy to create a visible form or a material object. The more energy required, the more difficult it is.
>
> We use more energy to materialize ourselves as more solid. There is a learning curve to affecting the

physical environment. To create things in the physical it is more difficult, requires a great deal of energy, and is not done very often.

We can also influence someone's physical body or thoughts with energy. We do that if there is a good reason for it. We must be greatly skilled to materialize or dematerialize objects. It takes a large amount of energy to do that.

How do spirits move things in the physical world?

My Guide:

We create energy or force that is able to direct or move objects.

Harvey's guides:

They move things by the equivalent of kinetic energy. They are pure energy. It is the same way a soprano can break a glass-sympathetic resonance. They concentrate a pure focus of their energy.

Spirits can affect the electric lights turning them on and off and make appliances work even when they're not plugged in. I've personally seen some of these things. If we're a Spirit in the human body, why can't we do it now?

My Guide:

When we die our Spirit senses are awakened, come into effect, and one aspect is greater control of our energy. Now on earth you are operating through your body and physical senses, which are an interface with your environment. You are limited by their capabilities.

You ask me what the difference in our senses is. We think more clearly. We find knowledge more accessible. Our perceptions are heightened, both visual and auditory. Our senses are more attuned. We don't have to process what we receive, that is, impressions, through a body and transfer them to our minds. We receive them directly, more fully, more rapidly, without interference, in a more expanded sense, perceiving more. It's like having a world opened up to you.

Our interpretations, assessment, and views, our desires and drives are still individual.

We have more power as spirits to influence, to transfer thoughts and impressions, to affect our environment.

We are greatly expanded in all regards. As we are energy, we have greater effect on energy as it pertains to the earth, but as we are non-physical, we have less ability to influence the physical. It is a skill we can learn and improve.

Harvey's guides:

Too much garbage. Trying to focus your thought on one pinpoint is difficult when we are in human form. There is too much going on to concentrate our energy.

It's a learned skill, but I don't think for spirits that it's that difficult.

Can spirits appear on earth momentarily in a true physical form?

My Guide:

If there is a great need for a physical manifestation of a spirit, it can be performed. We can be solid if we wish to on the earth plane. We can create a physical body for ourselves that is as solid to the touch as yours.

Once we cross over it is more difficult. If there is a great need for it, the energy will be provided us. We are able to appear visually and tactilely. It's not common, but it is possible under necessitating circumstances.

Can spirits ever come to earth temporarily in a physical body to help someone?

My Guide:

We are able to take on a body briefly for a purpose. We are able to do this because we are given the permission to help someone.

Harvey's guides:

I think it happens more often than not. As a spirit, if one of our loved ones is in trouble, we will help freely, without profit motive, or ego motive.

Sixty Three

Poltergeists

Are poltergeists created by the living or just mischievous ghosts?

My Guide:

They are created by the living. They are energy forms that are externalized and act on the environment. Some are very powerful.

However, a mischievous ghost or nonhuman entity that is powerful can reproduce the same phenomenon. So the answer is case dependent.

Physical phenomenon can have their origin in poltergeists or powerful malicious human or nonhuman spirits. Every case is different.

Harvey's guides:

I think they are spirits that are enabled by people that are living. The energy to move objects is from the living, triggered by spirits.

Laurie's Guides:

People do not create poltergeists. They are energy beings. They have a separate existence. They are energy beings that exist but not in this dimension. They are attracted to certain conditions, temporal anomalies such as an open portal, a frequency which may be appropriate for the energy of those beings. If you have a rift, they can come through. When a shaman or other religious individual comes, they use prayer or a ritual to remove them and to then close the portal.

Sixty Four

Portals

Can spirits be near the earth and do they have to go through portals to access the earth plane?

My Guide:

Yes, we do. We have to learn how to get through the dimensional barrier. Those of us who serve as guides have an open channel. Others can visit different places on earth but have to be able to breach the veil. This is accomplished through energy channels, vortexes, or portals.

Yes, they do go through portals. A channel is created for us to visit those on earth. It is a portal made available to us to make contact with our loved ones.

Those who dabble in the occult can create portals and there are natural portals or energetic gateways on the earth. Such a portal is an open door for spirits to go through, and allows spirits of all inclinations, both negative and positive, to pass indiscriminately.

Harvey's guides:

Yes and no. The only thing they really require is the energy request by the recipient. We create an energy field-our desire to commune with spirit is enough.

Yes, there are portals, but they seem to be more involved with negative spirits than positive spirits.

Sixty Five

Progression in the Afterlife

What is the benefit of advancement? Are there rewards like riches on earth?

My Guide:

Yes, we have advancement. Some souls are more advanced than others. The advancement is itself the benefit. They are more content, more peaceful. They have more joy, fulfillment, hope, and satisfaction. Their environment is one of greater harmony and bliss.

The change inside is the reward and that manifests outwardly in their environment and surroundings-ineffable joy, peace, and love. The environment around them-it is the reflection of their inner peace and joy.

Riches on earth are as much a burden as a reward. They can bring grief as much as contentment and do not assure happiness. They are a source of momentary satisfaction, not of true contentment, which comes from the heart, not from outside.

My quotation from the Bible, which states, "Store up your treasures in heaven where moth and rust do not corrupt; Be content in well doing", references that inner wealth.

Robert Brown, the British medium, said, "Progress is open to all."

What I have learned from the spirits is that what changes when we grow spiritually or especially when we get to the other side is awareness. Awareness of the spiritual nature of life and of our true purpose. It's like opening up a door to greater understanding.

Sixty Six

Progress on Earth

What can we do on earth to improve our progress in our lives?

My Guide:

Act in unselfishness. Show a genuine concern for others. Seek to treat others with the same consideration with which you wish to be treated.

Look at all situations from both perspectives. Consider how you would wish to be treated and treat others that way. Express and demonstrate love.

Do constructive work, learn, improve yourself, and share. Learn to treat yourself and others with respect. Act with integrity and honesty. Act in love toward all.

Harvey's guides:

Everybody does it differently. A beggar who has nothing and helps a blind man to cross the street does as much as a millionaire who gives half his fortune away. Recognition is not part of the reward.

Helpfulness with others, charity, treating different situations with love. Being a better person is the reward itself. We make mistakes but hopefully learn from them.

We do it every time we talk to someone else, every time we make ourselves available to them. When you're in a group and you speak against bigotry, it's just as important as buying a billboard.

Sixty Seven

Purpose

How can we discern our life's purpose while we are alive?

My Guide:

Look for repetitive patterns or problems in your life. Look for the issue that troubles you most. If you have a recurrent trouble that occupies your mind or that dragon you just can't seem to slay, that is a clue to your life's lesson. The general purpose of life is learning how to relate to others, how to cope with problems, finding the most prudent solutions and making the best choices.

Harvey's Guides:

The purpose of our life is universal- it is a school. We may have a life's plan but we may not follow it step-by-step.

I think fate or karma has a lot to do with that. Everyone knows what direction they want to go. It comes in our heart. It is an urge or burning, I should do this or want to do that.

Do we have a God-given purpose or intent that is unique to each of us?

My Guide:

We each have a purpose for which we were created-part of God's intent for our path/destiny. We realize our destiny as we increase our spiritual awareness.

We have a God-given plan for our lives and direction, suited to our individual personality and temperament. We are able to develop in that direction and provide help to others in their progression.

When we find our purpose and act in our purpose or truth, we are more in alignment with Source, and able to be used by Source. We each have that special purpose that is unique to our identity and each plays a part in the orchestra of God.

Harvey's guides:

Yes. And some fulfill it, some don't. That's where free choice comes into play. Not all of our choices are good.

Can you give me an overview of our purpose in incarnating and interpersonal relationships? Can you explain why those on the other side refer to our earth world as an illusion?

My Guide:

We call this world an illusion because it is a temporary reality. It is real to us while we experience it, but it is not the lasting permanent reality.

We come from a place where there is no hurt, no harm, no negativity, nothing but love, into a place where negativity and harm are possible, and happen to us.

We are free to experience negativity and harm, both to give and receive. We are here learning the lessons like baby spirits, about the values of Spirit-the love and kindness, and the only way that we can learn them when we have free will is to experience them ourselves. By experiencing the effects of negativity expressed upon ourselves, we come to understand not to perpetrate it on others. We learn to act unselfishly, kindly, and with love and compassion.

Harvey's guides:

We incarnate to learn more quickly. There are lessons we can learn on the physical plane that we cannot learn on the other side. Relationships we experience on the earth plane are for mutual growth.

How would you describe the overall purpose of all souls?

My Guide:

You can make decisions about life when you are on the earth. They are helpful to learn from. We come to earth after we decide what we need to learn. We follow our path that we predestined.

We made choices that would reflect our need to learn. Our choices were for purposes we currently don't understand. We made choices to learn from them. It's learning how to be positive when we don't live in a positive situation. We can't make everything perfect or right on the earth but we can learn to choose the best actions or alternatives possible in a negative situation.

We learn to attempt to avoid a negative situation or make the best choices possible if we can't avoid it. We are learning to make difficult choices that will make a difficult situation better. The choice involves leaving it, changing it, or coping with it in the best way possible.

We learn that once in a negative situation, with multiple interacting personalities, we cannot always avoid negative situations. We can attempt to avoid contributing to them with our choices, but as others are involved, we sometimes can only react in the best way possible.

We can't always solve or avoid the negative consequences we have incurred from others' actions, but we learn to correct or avoid our own mistakes and then make the best choices possible once in a negative predicament.

We are not perfect but we are learning to be better and to make better choices. Now we have to act in accordance with what we have learned. Every action starts as a thought. We are ultimately learning to solve issues, think more clearly, make better choices that result in better actions. So we work at improving our own understanding and consequently our own deeds.

Our ultimate purpose is learning to be a kinder, more caring, more loving soul. We all have our own unique issues we need to learn to address that are associated with our specific characteristics and personalities. Everyone has their own specific problems. We need to work on our weaknesses and difficulties.

As we work on these, they are no longer a factor in our problems. We can change ourselves because we choose to. I have changed and you will too. I learned from what I did wrong and the consequences.

It is about learning to make better, wiser decisions and interact better or be better partners with people, to improve our relations despite our differences, to act with more consideration, compassion, judiciousness, and less selfishness.

This does not mean that we are always required to be a victim. If we are suffering wrong at the hands of another, and we cannot compromise, sometimes we learn that the best option is to leave a situation.

We never end. We always are working on things, working toward perfection, learning wisdom by trial and error. There is a reason for our learning – to come into the understanding of truth – not just truth as told to us, but the knowledge of truth gained by experience.

There are choices, options, and alternatives that we each have as unique individuals, but behind these variations there are fundamental truths to discover about reality, relationships, choices, actions, and consequences, that we cannot understand unless we have lived through the spectrum of experiences, their consequences, and the outcome of our own actions upon ourselves and others, and of their actions upon themselves and us. We are living and learning the results of the actions and thoughts of our own and others, enabling us to choose those actions and thoughts that are positive, productive, and result in happiness for all concerned.

When we have learned these things we need not return to the situations to relearn them. They are a part of our permanent database of knowledge.

Our ultimate design or purpose is not given to us but is ours to discover. It is a knowing inside – a realization of our own specific path and purpose. We are co-creators with Source in our manifestation of truth and light, to live, effect, and demonstrate truth and light in our individual actions. Our purpose may vary based upon our inherent nature, personality, and skill set, but in its individual variance, it is always meant to produce good, to produce beauty and the betterment of ourselves and others.

So there is not one purpose, but many, all with a single truth at their core – the betterment and progress of the soul in its achievements, its creative pursuits, its productivity, and its relations with other creating souls– to create together a world or environment of light, love, happiness, and spiritual beauty and joy in love for all.

We are all going to be in "heaven", the abode of God, if we choose to. No one will be excluded ultimately unless they want to be or their choices do not permit them to be there. It is a matter of their free will.

It is not within the comprehension of mortal man. It is more than we are able to understand. It is for us to know as we grow toward perfection. As we improve our understanding we see more.

When we were children we did not see all the things we grew to see as adults because we were learning. Also we now are learning. We are on a ladder of spiritual maturation – of growth, attainment of spiritual understanding and ideals. We are able to see as much as our vision and experience permits at any given time.

The truth is there for us when we are able to apprehend it and we as the director of our education and future are able to initiate our course, or lessons, and our progress. We are creating the opportunities and providing the willingness and effort to learn and those opportunities will be provided us as we choose to face them, embrace them, learn and develop from them.

As such, we are the authors of our future selves. We have accomplished what we have chosen to accomplish and are moving forward to accomplish more in an ever ascending path of understanding, peace, joy, and love that has no end, but returns to God or Source with the attainments and wisdom of each soul's experiences. We will learn forever, each soul fulfilling its own separate destiny, in the perfect plan of God, the one, the each in the many, the separate in the grand network, plan, the perfect purpose, plan and design of God.

Sixty Eight

Readjustment to the Afterlife

When we return to the afterlife do we have to make an adjustment or do we instantaneously revert to the way we were before we came to earth?

My Guide:

> We have to process what we went through in our lives. We need some time to adjust. We have a clearer picture of what we planned and did and did not accomplish.
>
> You have to get used to it again. We need to readjust to being in spirit and not in a body. Most find it easy. Some have a difficult time with it.
>
> All need some adjustment and there are those who help us through the process.

Harvey's Guides:

There is a period of transition- a greeting room.

Question: if we've had multiple lives, why do we need to be "shown the ropes" on the other side when we return?

My Guide:

We need to be re-oriented-like when a piece of jewelry has weathered and tarnished, it needs to be polished. Or if you've moved away from your old home and lived somewhere else for many years, when you come back you forgot many things, and others have changed, and you need to be re-acquainted and familiarized to feel comfortable.

Harvey's guides:

We have selective amnesia. When we come over, we forget what we had on the other side. When we were sent back here, we retain some of the knowledge we had on the other side. That's why we're all so different.

But if we recalled everything or knew everything that was going on on the other side or if we knew that everything was so much better, we couldn't function. We might all go stand in front of a bus to get back there. This is a learning experience.

Sixty Nine

Reality versus Illusion

Is our experience in the spirit world merely a dream or fantasy or are we actually interacting with other spirits and do we have real rather than imagined surroundings?

My Guide:

> The spirit world is real, not just an imaginary fantasy or dream.

Harvey's guides:

> Spirit is not just a dream or product of the imagination. It is real. Every time you contact them you find out how real it is.

Is the spirit world just a dream or fantasy? Is it just part of our imagination or is it real? Do we actually see the people we love or just imagine them?

My Guide:

It's not a dream. It's a real existence. The material things are not here. It depends on how advanced we are. If we do manifest a body, we can have clothing, jewelry, anything we had on earth. We don't have a need for material things, most of which are used for maintaining or adorning a physical body.

Without a need to eat, sleep, provide a living, raise children, or maintain a home, the material pursuits and labors which occupy us on earth are largely abnegated. Since we don't have a body to maintain, a house to purchase, or a need to provide for the physical well-being of other souls, most of the time occupying pursuits and obligations of the earth is no longer relevant.

We are real. We are not a fantasy, dream, or imaginary world, but priorities are different from those on earth.

Harvey's guides:

Initially we do contact them in the form that we remember them. As we go higher and higher in the spirit world, we no longer need to see them in the same form that we recall.

It's not a make-believe world. It's real.

Quite often we are greeting people who preceded us. Yes, actually, a lot of times Spirit leaves before the body shuts down.

You can be comforted by your loved ones at the time of your death.

Is there an objective reality in the spirit world? Are there real objects perceived by yourself and others?

My Guide:

The answer is a conundrum or oxymoron. It is a "puzzle wrapped up in a mystery", because it is like the old question, do we have free will?

Ethical relativists say we have free will to do what we will, but we do not have free will to will what we will, because what we will is dependent upon our inborn personality and imprinted environment. In other words, we cannot objectively stand apart from ourselves and will something because our will is a prisoner, influenced by our innate inborn personality and the influence we have accepted or been subjected to by our environment.

In the same manner, life after death is an objective reality but it is predicated on our individual subjective thoughts and desires, which manifest themselves as reality. Therefore, life after death is our subjective reality that becomes objective to us.

As Gretchen Vogel put it, the afterlife is a self-directed mental reality.

As on the earth, your wish creates the behavior that will help you attain it.

Harvey's guides:

Things in the spirit world are thoughts. They are visualized and as real as you make them.

I asked whether this means they are an illusion or fantasy in the mind or whether they are external and real.

The answer was, it depends on what you consider an illusion.

After I asked whether houses can exist in the spirit world, the guides said that you can visualize houses and inhabit them the same way as you would on earth.

Laurie's guides:

Your thoughts. That's how you create things in the afterlife and they actually exist. There are buildings in the afterlife. When you create something others can see it. There is a shared external reality. There are various realities in the afterlife. Some live in houses in the afterlife. There are many places like that. To them, this earth world is an illusion.

There are different realities based upon different needs, levels, developments, and desires. The same thing is true on earth. The afterlife is not a punishment. If you create your own home, it will be there for you to see and for others to see. You create what you want.

Question: is this present physical world reality?

My Guide:

This world is not reality. It is a temporary physical reality created for the purpose of learning. The ultimate and lasting reality is the world of spirit. The visualized world is made possible for a learning experience.

Why do some on the other side think of this earth as an illusion?

My Guide:

Because we don't see the full picture of our purpose and spiritual life. We don't see the whole truth.

Harvey's guides:

No. It's not. It's every bit as real as all the other levels of the afterlife, just another step on the way.

Why do spirits describe the earth life as an illusion?

My Guide:

The physical life, material things, the physical body, fame, and other ego driven pursuits are illusory because they are temporal, temporary, and not a permanent reality. That is why they say people are always chasing illusions. It is real to us while we experience it, but it is not the lasting permanent reality.

Seventy

Reincarnation

Do you believe in reincarnation?

When I went to my first mediumship class I felt very inadequate. It felt like a coincidence that I got in, but in retrospect I suspect it wasn't. One of the readings I got from Robert Brown was of my loved one and guide in spirit carrying a huge pile of books. Those were the lessons I've been encountering. Thanks to spirit I also got a huge heap of presents, gifts helping me to develop clairaudience, clairvoyance and clairsentience. They generously helped me through that first seminar and never let me fall on my face.

My Guide:

> I have been reincarnated multiple times. It's my choice to be reincarnated because I can learn the lessons my soul needs to learn. I can't do it as effectively in the afterlife. The earth is mostly a big school. It's all lessons.

Harvey's Guides:

Yes. What you've learned on the earth plane determines your direction next time around.

Can you give me an overview of our purpose in incarnating and interpersonal relationships?

My Guide:

We come from a place where there is no hurt, no harm, no negativity, nothing but love, into a place where negativity and harm are possible, and happen to us.

We are free to experience negativity and harm, both to give and receive. We are here learning the lessons like baby spirits, about the values of Spirit-the love and kindness, and the only way that we can learn them when we have free will is to experience them ourselves. By experiencing the effects of negativity expressed upon ourselves, we come to understand not to perpetrate it on others. We learn to act unselfishly, kindly, and with love and compassion.

Harvey's guides:

We incarnate to learn more quickly. There are lessons we can learn on the physical plane that we cannot learn on the other side. Relationships we experience on the earth plane are for mutual growth.

Can a soul incarnate whenever it wants to and incarnate by itself?

My Guide:

We don't incarnate by ourselves because we incarnate to learn lessons, and thus must plan our earth lives with other souls with that purpose in mind. So we incarnate in groups to achieve that purpose.

We can incarnate outside of a group if we have others who are willing to embrace us.

The decision about when to incarnate is never solely ours. It is decided by the group and if a soul wishes to abstain and remain on the other side, they can.

Harvey's guides:

Usually souls do not incarnate singly, but in a group. Also, they cannot incarnate at any time just because they want to. It is a mutual decision.

Does God ever tell us when or how to reincarnate or do we choose?

My Guide:

Most of us choose to go back so that we can learn a lesson more expeditiously than we can on the other side. Some of us are requested by God through emissaries, teachers, and leaders, to go back specifically for a purpose or needed lesson.

Each soul has its own journey. As we become closer to Source, we are more aware of our interaction with Source. It's a blend. We do have free will but God does provide guidance and advice. It depends on whether we are willing to listen to it.

A soul is not forced to develop, to incarnate, or incarnate in a specific manner, but the needs of a soul may cause it to incarnate more rapidly or into a certain environment or lifetime that will further its progress. So the answer is yes, and yes. We do have free will but we have a larger purpose that influences our decisions and restrictions depending upon our past performance and development.

Is there anything you would like to tell people about the nature of the afterlife?

My Guide:

When you get discouraged here, remember that the accomplishments you made in your lifetime are not always recognized until you get here. What you may see as failures are just as important as what the world regards as successes. If you have learned from something, good or bad, and are the wiser for it, you have benefitted.

Harvey's Guides:

As we get closer to incarnation, part of what we learned in our last life is imparted into our brain. This is very important in order to advance, as on the earth plane what we learned in the past lives will make us better people.

Is there any trans- species reincarnation? Do dogs progress and become human? Do we reincarnate as a worm or a lion?

My Guide:

We do not have a reincarnation into another species. People do not reincarnate as dogs, and dogs do not reincarnate as people. They develop as we do and progress through learning and the earthly experience.

Do we plan our lives and make choices about what family we will be born into, who we will associate with, and what we will do for a career, or are there restrictions or limitations on our plans?

My Guide:

It's all for a purpose. The plans must coincide with our overall purpose, and must benefit our growth in areas of our individual weakness.

As long as other souls agree to make these exchange contracts with us, and both souls can achieve the lesson they desired to learn by the incarnation, those plans can be effected.

The relationships, careers, and events must serve a purpose to help us learn and grow in the needed areas.

Harvey's guides:

When we plan our lives we are pointed in a certain direction by more advanced spirits.

Seventy One

Reincarnation versus Ascension

Do we have a choice regarding whether we wish to reincarnate or ascend? Is it our choice alone or do we need to have approval from more advanced souls directing us? Do we have to reincarnate with our soul group or can we reincarnate apart from them?

My Guide:

> We are not forced to reincarnate. We are very much encouraged to reincarnate to speed up our learning. We do have choices.
>
> We can ascend but must reach a certain level of attainment before we do. Spiritual assessments and others more advanced determine our eligibility. We don't have to incarnate because we can stay in the afterlife, but we don't learn as rapidly.

We can decide to reincarnate or ascend, but we must receive permission from higher authorities before we do either. We have free will within the framework of spiritual hierarchy.

Harvey's guides:

Some would reincarnate. Some would just rise. I'll probably reincarnate-I have a lot to give. That's how we pay our dues.

Is there a time when souls don't have to reincarnate on earth and ascend in the afterlife? What level no longer needs to reincarnate?

My Guide:

Yes, we have a time when we no longer have to incarnate. We can incarnate even after that if we do so for humanitarian purposes.

We are not told we have to incarnate. We are given the option. Most souls prefer to incarnate for the greater learning opportunities.

Once we become a much stronger soul and have control of our hearts, desires, and minds, and are committed to living a good and altruistic life, we no longer need to reincarnate.

We both need to create a stronger inner control and direction, and need to reincarnate as a means of proof of our learned lessons that we have established control over our impulses, that the spirit man has power over the earthly man. That's why we both need to reincarnate again.

We do so for the greater rapidity of progress. Once we have reached the fifth level of attainment, reincarnation is performed for help to others rather than for modification and polishing of self.

Does God send us back or do we choose to come back?

My Guide:

God may encourage us to return to earth for a purpose, but we are involved in the particulars. We are given a mission, but we have choice in how we wish to accomplish that mission.

Harvey's guides:

We have a choice. I don't think there is any force involved in it. There are people that are far advanced, Mother Teresa, Rosa Parks, with no ulterior motives and they are willing to sacrifice for the good of others, and that also exists on the other side.

That may have been a direction she was headed from the beginning. If God directed everything it would be very restrictive.

Seventy Two

Relationships

When we are on earth we have some relatives that we are closer to, some people that we get along better with. We have some people that we love more than others. Do we love all others equally on the other side? For instance, will a mother love her brutal and abusive ex-husband equally with her adored child? Will a woman love someone who raped and murdered her child as much as her devoted husband? Do we still love and bond more deeply with some souls on the other side as we do on earth?

My Guide:

We do have some we are closer to on the other side. We have some that we are more fond of than others. Preferences remain.

We have some that we love very dearly and others we are not close to. You don't have a chance to act out the negative qualities, so we have more love for one another. We aren't angry because there are no anger provoking situations. It's a peaceful environment that promotes love and understanding.

We have some we are very close to and others we are not, but we have a general respect and love for all, a love of kindly concern.

We don't have the same amount of personal attraction or love for all that are here. We have some that we are much closer to than others, with whom we have more affinity. Some have a much deeper bond of love between them than others, some have a stronger connection. Some we see seldom or not at all.

We do want the best for one another and try to help each other and appreciate one another.

We have different levels and degrees of love based on compatibility and interpersonal attraction of temperament, personality, and goals-having different affinities as like attracts like. It's similar to earth, but not based on physical attraction, but inner soul attraction, the lasting and true attraction that draws people together or separates them. Some are more harmonious than others. Some have true and lasting companionship.

We know each other and understand each other and when we love someone we love them for who they really are-an affinity of soul. A bond that is more lasting and permanent. True love is never broken.

Harvey's guides:

People are different and still have preferences on the other side.
When I asked the guides whether you would be equally close to or equally love someone who was abusive and harmed you as a beloved child they answered:

Absolutely not. It is not important to be with them. We forgive each other and walk away.

That's why we talk about hell. We create our own personal hell on earth when we are with someone abusive or incompatible. Why would you ever want to be united with someone who abused you?

Yes, you still pick and choose.

In the spirit world do we retain our individual identity, and as in the physical world, do we love some more than others, will we be closer to some than we are to others?

My Guide:

We are able to be closer to some than to others. We have a much deeper attachment to some than we do to others.

We all have different attributes and predilections. We have some that we care for much more than others in a personal sense, not in a godly sense. We have some souls we are more attached to and some we love more deeply than others.

If we have had a bad relationship with someone on earth, we make peace with each other, discuss what we were supposed to learn from one another, and leave, go our separate ways.

Not all souls spend equal amounts of time together. We have some that see themselves as couples.

We are very similar to the way we were before-just more loving. We all are different. None of us are alike. We have our own traits. We have our own individual identity. Some souls are closer, more compatible, and love each other more than others. Some souls love each other more than others because of who they are inside.

Harvey's guides:

Yes, but not the way we know it on earth. As you ascend through the levels, physical contact is not as important to you and you can have purer thoughts. Physical contact is not necessary at the higher levels.

Some souls are closer than others. However, love is different, because there is no pressure to impress other people. As we get closer and closer to Source, some of the drives that we had on earth no longer exist.

We can have a deeper attachment to some than others in a spiritual sense. In the lower levels, yes, some souls love one another more as we do on earth. As you go higher and higher love is less earth-like and more spiritual.

What are the determining factors in how closely we relate with individual souls on the other side?

My Guide:

We have love for each other in the sense that we want to see each other succeed, we want to see each other progress. We practice kindness, consideration, and compassion. We have a concern for each other's welfare and development.

We do not love each other equally as a partner, to live with, to be a companion, or to marry. We have different interests, goals, personalities, and temperaments. We have some that we are closer to than others. We join others that we have more in common with-the agreement and harmony of like minds. We love some in a sense that we have intense and deep communion, unity, and compatibility with them. We can have a deep love, joy, togetherness, and commitment with them-a unity and union of minds and souls.

Harvey's guides:

Some souls have more affinity than others, and they are the ones who stay closer together. Those who are more like each other are closer.

What is it that governs spiritual attraction? Are there spiritual couples?

My Guide:

Even if all negative behavior were eliminated, we still have preferences, because we are all individuals, and some, because of unique temperament and desires, will be closer physically and spiritually than others.

This is because we have many choices within the spectrum of acceptable behavior. We have some whose minds are so similar and love is so deep, they are unified with one another. It is like super glue that binds some together, while others are different and choose a different path. It is spiritual and mental affinity that unites us.

Even if we forgive one another, that doesn't necessarily make us more compatible. It just makes us kinder in our behavior toward one another-able to get along more harmoniously.

We still have individual differences and preferences as well as character traits of our personalities that draw us to be more compatible, more peaceful, closer, more harmonious, more simpatico, more similar in our thinking, interests, values and personality, more happy with some than with others. Simply put, we have more affinity with some souls than with others.

Even if all the negatives of our behavior are eliminated, we still are different, and those likenesses and affinities draw us to be together with some and not with others. And on that basis, we will have degrees of closeness and levels of companionship.

Harvey's guides:

Yes, we do have closer relationships with some souls than with others.

Are there relationships in the spirit world?

Laurie's guides:

There are relationships in the spirit world-categorically. There are, because there are people who want to be "married" or make a commitment to each other.

Interpersonal or inter- soul relationships on the other side

Laurie's guides:

There are still some people who see themselves as couples on the other side. There are also spirits who prefer being a male or female in appearance, and some who are androgynous.

There are some people who are closer together on the other side. Some don't see each other at all.

Some get together to work out their issues, forgive each other, and then part.

Souls can remain together if they have similar attributes, world views, and interests. Those with the deepest bond of love don't part.

They can make commitments with each other. These are spiritual commitments. They can be referred to as unions.

What is the essence of the spiritual bond of companionship, of pairing?

My Guide:

Although we retain our individual identities we become one in our love, one in our mutual support, one in our concerns, one in our efforts and mutual endeavors, one in our future shared growth, and one in our commitment to one another.

Can you say a few things about the compatibility between two people?

My Guide:

We all have our own vision and our own direction. We have values that we embrace. When two people are aligned in their thinking, they are happy.

When they have similar emotional, physical, spiritual, and intellectual viewpoints, or character, they are compatible.

These shared qualities produce unity, companionship, compatibility, and bonding. These produce harmony, contentment, peace, joy, fulfillment, and a thriving relationship in which two partners have entered a path together to shape their mutual future growth, accomplishments, happiness, and unity.

Harvey's guides:

As on Earth, some have shared or common interests, goals, and preferences.

What is the difference between those who are united in spirit and those who are connected in spirit?

My Guide:

We see those who are connected as those who are affiliated by prior experiences. You are connected with someone through your shared experiences.

Union is a voluntary spiritual agreement of two deeply loving souls to remain closely allied and is entered into as a declaration or commitment, not merely as the outcome or byproduct of prior shared experiences. Union is a matter of volition and desire for a shared continuing close relationship, an ongoing bond in which souls express their wish to remain together on their journey.

Harvey's guides:

Those who are connected are those who have had shared or mutual experiences together but have not made a commitment to be united.

Relationships on the other side

My Guide:

We have no worries after we get across. There are no problems that we worry about. We have so much joy here. There is no comparison. Our lives are much easier and more fulfilling.

No one has the same difficulties we had on earth. I don't have the same problems. No one does. We just talk to people about what happened to us and make some amends. We don't have the same irritations we had on earth.

Sometimes we get angry but not often. It's not something we do normally. Once we get to the other side we realize why we were with a person. We don't have to be around someone just because we were in our lifetime. There are some people we wish to be around and others we don't. There are people we have close relationships with and others who are more distant.

We are able to forgive each other and not be so upset with each other. We don't have to be with each other but we can. It depends on the people.

People who had difficulties with each other during their lives discuss their problems, make peace, and a more harmonious relationship with each other, but don't typically stay with each other or stay together. They often part ways and become better people for the experience. We don't stay together with those we don't have a deep love for. We have some we are close to and some we are not.

We become more kind, caring, and considerate but we move on, and don't stay together. We don't stay with people we didn't get along with on earth. We move on. We have our own lives. We act pleasant and cordial when we do see them. We have differences, and we don't have to be with those who are of a different mind.

Our deep love for one another keeps us together. No one makes us stay with someone we were with on earth. It's all up to us. If we had a good relationship, we might stay.

People are all like they were on earth – different, with different ideas and desires. No one has the same identical personality as another. We don't stay with someone because we were with them on earth.

We live with those we are closest to, with whom we have the deepest understanding and love. When people were unhappy together, they don't normally stay together. They often part and go their own ways.

People gravitate towards those they have most in common with. People don't spend the same amount of time with all souls. They spend most time with those they are closest to. It's like Earth. There are some we are very close to and want to be with all the time, and others we don't care to spend time with.

We lose our anger and reconcile our differences. We become more accepting and don't fight. We make peace with someone and go our own ways. We don't have to be around them or see them. We just are pleasant when we do. We bear no grudge. We forgive, live, and let live.

We can love each other as souls and have a regard for each other, but it doesn't mean we want to be together, live together, or be married to one another. We don't have to want to be with someone. We just wish them well and appreciate what we have learned from them. We don't have to live with them or be with them. It's just a common regard we have for one another. We learn to be harmonious. We don't bear grudges or ill will. We learn to love people because we wish for their progress or well-being.

We don't stay with someone we don't love as a partner or companion. We stay with those we love as companions, with whom we have a deep love. We love others in the sense that we wish for their forward momentum, their progress, and their well-being. We appreciate the lessons we learned from them and wish them well. We love them as souls that we wish well for, who have touched our lives. We wish them well, then depart and go our own way. We don't necessarily wish to stay with them, be with them, or be around them. We have some we wish to be happy, and others we wish to be with.

We have some we have deeper bonds of love with that we wish to be with, to live with, or be married to.

Others we don't have a deep bond of love with, and wish them well and wish them happiness.

We are not all partners. We have separate relationships with each soul. Some of us are close and some are not. But we wish all well. We have love for souls because we want them to be happy and to learn. We have regard, acceptance, and an altruistic love. But we have some that we have a different feeling for. We have some that we wish to marry or to be with us. We have some that we have a very close bond of love with and others who come and go.

We choose to remain with some souls as partners, companions, friends, in deeply loving unions. Those are our partners, our companions, who are inseparable, who are our closest loved ones and comrades, companions. Some are so close we choose not to leave them. They are our mates, our partners, our companions, partners who are one soul, one heart. They are our closest in love, our deepest bonds, our spiritual commitments. They are the closest relationship one can have, more than a wife or husband, an unsevered companion of the soul.

One heart, one mind, one soul – a union that is more close than any other. The deepest bond, the deepest love. Two hearts that become one. Two souls that are both now and forever united.

Relationship Advice

My Guide:

There is an old saying. Don't go to bed angry. No one is perfect except God. We inevitably will hurt each other and make mistakes. If we feel a relationship is worth having, we must both be willing to forgive one another, compromise and change.

We have to forgive each other our mistakes, but not just that. We must then restore our previous affection, excitement, happiness, and communication, or the relationship will grow apart. A wall will divide us. And it will grow into an insurmountable wall. It will create a distance between the two that will grow into a chasm that cannot be bridged. If the two parties have discovered that they are not compatible, then co-existence that is achieved will only be a truce, a compromise, and artificial acquiescence without true fulfillment.

The previous harmony and excitement must be restored or it will lead to indifference, a wall, and a division. Both parties have to be willing to give and work on it. One cannot do it alone if the other refuses. If this is the case, the one will look for gratification elsewhere, leave, or suffer in silence and just live in a dead relationship.

No matter how good the relationship, it must be nourished by both individuals or die. Both must be willing to commit, change, compromise, and endeavor to keep up the vitality of the relationship.

When we come to the earth we don't know what we are going to encounter. We learn from our mistakes so we don't have to repeat them again. Two people are responsible for the outcome, not one. We can only control our own actions and behaviors, not that of others.

We should be cautious before we enter into a relationship with many obligations. We should examine it and learn from what we see before making a commitment that affects us and others. We can only protect ourselves to a degree from deception on the part of another. We can talk things out before hand, evaluate what we both want from and expect in a relationship and examine the behavior of the other.

Do their actions match their promises? See if they are willing to put their money where their mouth is. Check what they show before making the commitment. See what they do. Weigh the negatives and positives. Are you willing to live with the flaws? How do you harmonize? Are you compatible? Do you complement and support one another? Is there a basis for trust? How do you handle the difficult situations together? Is there unity or disparity? Is there love or friction? You know in your heart if you love this person for better or worse. If they aren't the right person for you, move on before taking on responsibilities and entanglements.

Otherwise your life will be an unhappy compromise at best and a term of imprisonment at worst.

You must weigh the pros and cons of change. If there are many serious adverse consequences to changing you must accept the consequences of living in a long-term unhappy relationship. Sometimes the choice is between the lesser of two evils. There is no neat answer. It depends on the consequences you are willing to live with. Major financial investments and obligations, dependents, or physical disabilities may present large barriers to surmount in leaving a situation, and if the incentives for leaving are not strong enough, we may suffer for years as a result of our previous decisions.

If this is the case, we need to look for a purpose or redeeming factor to sustain our drive, to soldier on until we can be free of our burdens. The strength comes from inside, from the indefatigable spirit that gives us hope for a new start and for the wisdom to try our options and hopefully make better decisions the next time. Perhaps there is something to say for the show me person from Missouri.

Seventy Three

Religion

Are there different environments we go to in the afterlife based on our religious or cultural beliefs and expectations, or is there one objective reality? Are there any vestiges of the major earthly religions in the afterlife?

My Guide:

If people are very set in their beliefs they may be blinded to greater realities. They may construct the environment of their vision. We have options, and if that is important to some, they may desire to continue with their earthly convictions or ideology.

If they come over with an open mind they will be free to take advantage of all the possibilities for growth that the afterlife offers.

If some have deep set beliefs they may choose to congregate with others of a similar mindset. There are various habitats in the afterlife created by like-minded souls. We often choose to associate or dwell with those of a similar mindset, similar goals, similar ideas and values. "Like attracts like in the law of the universe."

Just as those who share a deep or intense personal bond or commitment of love choose to be companions and remain close together, those of a similar character and vision more frequently associate.

Harvey's guides:

There can be on the lower levels. Vestiges of earthly religion as we ascend become less and less important.

Laurie's guides:

You do have churches in certain parts of level III but it is more like a gathering of people of similar minds, a philosophical sharing. All are one in the afterlife. Any earth trappings of religion are removed. Things that separate us out are lost.

Seventy Four

Right and Wrong

Why is it that some authors say that those on the other side say that there is no right or wrong? How can that be the case when they say there is ascension, levels, and progression through the levels? If there is progression and there are lessons there must be something to progress to, and something to learn. If there is no right and wrong, then a mass murderer, a child molester, a rapist, a serial killer, and a dictator practicing torture and genocide would be the same as Jesus, Gandhi, Buddha, Mohamed, Confucius, and Mother Teresa. There would be no need to learn or progress if there is no right and wrong. Then why not just murder, kill, steal, rape and destroy? If there is no right and wrong there's no reason not to. If there is no right or wrong, there's no need for a lesson or for progression.

My Guide:

We all need to look at our own lives and decide what is right or wrong based on our experiences. We live in a world where there are so many choices and we really are seeking the best options.

We learn by trial and error what the best choices are for us. No one can do the things that we call wrong on the other side. When you act out of compassion, unselfishness, self-sacrifice, kindness, love, generosity, forgiveness, charity, concern for the welfare of others, you are acting in a framework of godly love.

Penny, when we come to the other side we can't do these things-hurtful things. We learn to keep the good things in our heart. We are given so many truths within the world and we seek the answers out for ourselves. When we choose to act in accordance with the principles of the other side, unconditional love, we have then learned the lessons of the earth life.

What does love do? Love is patient, love is kind, love is forgiving, love is charitable, love is helpful and does good works, love manifests itself in caring deeds. It reaches out to others and is not self absorbed. We learn to control the negative emotions, selfishness, greed, intolerance, hatred, violence, harm, lies, injustice, falsehood, trucebreaking, fear, jealousy, wrath.

When we act in accordance with unconditional love, we have accomplished our purpose-from our experiences we learn negative from positive, results that lift up, not tear down, that help, not harm.

We learn to be in agreement with the principles of God - unconditional love.

Right and wrong are determined by our earthly experiences and can vary from culture to culture, are subjective in the eyesight of mankind.

There is that which is in concert with the atmosphere of the other side of unconditional love and benevolence, and it is through our own individual experiences that we learn to think, desire, and act in a manner in agreement, in accordance with those attributes, those principles.

That is as close as I can get it. No one will see the whole truth until they are in the realm of God that is called enlightenment and we must each find it for ourselves. Until it is incorporated in our heart, proclaimed on our tongue, and enacted in our deeds, it is not real to us.

The kingdom of God is within you. It is not a place-you are in the kingdom of God when you live a life of peace, joy, and love.

Laurie's guides:

Bullshit. When they say there is no right or wrong, it is not referring to the earth plane. On the other side when they say there is no right or wrong they mean that there are various learning opportunities and requirements and there may be a difference of opinion. There is no right or wrong learning situation.

Yes, in the lower realms, there can be negative behavior or bad behavior on the other side.

As far as our perception of wrong on the earth goes, there are multiple answers for different individuals of what may be right or wrong and multiple options fall within that realm. There are no absolutes.

There are many things that are wrong and many things in between. What is right or wrong can never be fully exposed on this side. In the afterlife we can find out what's expected.

We do not know everything when we return to the afterlife instantly. Why would we have ascending levels if we knew everything when we went there? We would just go to the top.

We can know the truth to a degree. You must seek and find your own truth.

There are many transgressions on the earth. They only apply on the earth plane. They apply on the other side only as a way to evaluate the lessons that need to be learned.

It is not that there is no right or wrong on the other side; it's that it doesn't occur there-it only occurs on the earth plane.

Negative thoughts and emotions can't hurt someone on the other side. Only actions do and harmful actions are not possible there. Not until they realize the hurt and injustice they create can souls truly progress.

Why do we need to learn lessons on earth about right and wrong if we can't do wrong on the other side?

My Guide:

Wisdom is based on understanding. Source wants us to embrace positive choices with free will and we must learn to choose the positive when we are in an environment of free will in order to put Source's laws into our heart.

Harvey's guides:

On earth we give examples to those around and we also demonstrate consequences for our behavior. Yes, even in the afterlife lessons are important because we can impart our knowledge to those who will be reincarnated.

Would you want a husband who chose not to cheat on you or one who didn't cheat only because he couldn't? God wants us to desire to do positive things of our own free will, not because we have to.

Seventy Five

Satan

Is there a lake of fire or Satan?

My Guide:

There is the spirit that we were refer to as Satanic in the negative behavior and desires of souls-any negative intentions or behavior may be referred to as Satanic. There is a Satanic force or ideology.

Spiritual force can be used for negative purposes or for good. "Satan" is not so much a specific soul as the principle of evil, embodied in many souls. Some are more powerful than others. They can be extremely powerful if they have strength to change peoples' minds or hearts.

Harvey's guides:

There is no such thing as a lake of fire. No, Satan is of our own making.

Seventy Six

Sex/Merging/ Affection/Intimacy

Can we express affection by hugging and kissing each other on the lower levels of the afterlife?

My Guide:

We can kiss and hug as we had on earth. It is a matter of retaining a physical type of body which we temporarily inhabit. We can reenact all of the sensations we had on Earth, including kissing and hugging, as well as passionate love.

We also can create the sensation of love by recalling the memories of experiences we had on the earth and reliving those sensations. We do that in a soul to soul fashion and can incorporate that type of feeling into the merging experience.

Harvey's guides:

Since they are at the lower levels, they still retain a vestige of the life we had on earth. The answer is yes, because we still can retain a vestige of our physical body, so we can still kiss like we did on earth.

You can also draw on memories and re-create the experience of kissing and it will be real to you.

Hopefully we retain some of our emotions, especially the positive ones, and can bring them up to the higher levels. Otherwise our earth experience would be an exercise in futility.

Laurie's guides:

You can have a physical body of higher vibration and kiss on the lower levels, or as you advance, you can access your memory bank and re-create all the sensation of a kiss between you. It will feel like a real kiss to you.

Is there sex on the other side?

My Guide:

We can make a body with our thoughts and re-create the feelings of sex. It is not necessary to go through the human physiologic processes and mechanisms, but we can directly experience the sensations we desire.

We can create the sensation of touch with our thoughts and create a body with which to experience it.

We can feel the feelings we would with a kiss, but we also can create the feelings we have through touching and hugging and experience them when we are in a bodily form.

It is feeling with our thoughts. Sight is present, hearing, and touch are present, but no longer conveyed through sensory organs, but directly through vibration. We can replicate the earthly senses by a different mechanism and establish a vehicle that mimics or is like the earthly body in which to experience our sensations.

The thoughts and feelings conveyed by the mind are direct, and we do not need the senses as we did on earth to engender those feelings, but we can have a replica of our earthly body if we wish.

How do spirits express affection or intimacy?

My Guide:

If we want to have a body we can do what we did on earth, experience affection by kissing, hugging, and touching. But we can also experience affection with an exchange of our thoughts, feelings, and emotions.

We can combine our thoughts and energies and become one. We call it merging. It's combining or blending our energies. We experience a complete awareness of each other. We unite our minds in the same way we united our bodies on earth and experience a great amount of intense passion and love.

We reach a height of love and intimacy we can't attain on earth-a spiritual nakedness and union-a complete sharing and union of two consciousnesses. It is like the dance of the seven veils. We remove each veil until we are fully known.

Harvey's guides:

At the lower levels, spirits experience affection and intimacy in a manner similar to what we have on earth, touch and affection.

As we ascend, it becomes less and less necessary for physical contact. Instead we can project thought and emotion.

If we desire contact, two energies can blend. It is a combination of senses. We can blend without physical contact by a blending of thoughts, feelings, and memories at the snap of a finger. We can project emotions from one to the other.

Can spirits re-create the experience of sexual activity in the afterlife? What is merging?

My Guide:

We can create a body for ourselves and react the way we would have reacted on earth. We have the power to re-create that feeling. It's like coming close to someone and blending with or sensing their energy. It's analogous to the earthly touch.

We can create a body that is like the one we had on earth and we can touch, hug each other, shake hands, and kiss like we would have on earth. We sense the touch with our mind. We make that sense come alive.

We can re-create the sexual experience as it was on earth. It's more intense than we had on earth because it's without the interruption or transport of the nervous system. It is direct, mind to mind- like an electrical explosion of bliss.

When we merge, our energy, thoughts, and minds become one. It is the most intimate experience you can have. It is becoming one temporarily. It's joy, bliss, and complete emotional rapture.

Harvey's guides:

In the lower realms-yes. They do retain memory. They can re-create the sensations if they want it, including some of their personality. They can re-create it in the afterlife.

Merging is becoming one- two souls, one thought, one meaning.

Can spirits have sex, or how do they show intimacy?

My Guide:

We can have sex. Many do not want sex because we have a more spiritual method of sharing affection and intimacy. How do souls share closeness, intimacy and bonding? We can be closer than those on earth.

We have deeper ties of love than we do on earth. We can share feelings more clearly and express feeling to one another in which the other soul feels our emotions. We both create our own feelings of joy, love, and intense excitement. It is a complete immersion in one another, a oneness where two souls have a deep spiritual love for each other. We can create thrills even deeper than sex with our intense thoughts and feelings for one another. We do have merging. Love and extreme rapture/bliss in one another.

It is like having the most intense feelings of bliss, joy, and rapture all-in-one. It's greater than the greatest sex you could have. We can have sex if we want it. We are able to make love. We will have that opportunity. It's a desire of the heart, not the body. We can have sex. We create the intense excitement of sex and the exhilaration with our thoughts.

We also can merge into each other and temporarily become one soul, but this involves the higher passions of love, respect, tenderness, and caring. It's like all the emotions you've ever had flood you at once.

It's a heightened sense of joy, peace, beauty, and sublimity. It's an explosion of beautiful feelings almost indescribable. It's even more exciting than the pinnacle of sex. It's so exciting you are almost incandescent.

Harvey's guides:

The simplest explanation is merging of spirits.

The same way some people with a pure voice break a glass-it's called sympathetic resonance. They vibrate at the same frequency.

Laurie's Guides:

God is a good creator. If two souls agree that they need something it will be provided for them. Bullshit. Disagree. Why would god have created sex if it were bad? God wouldn't deny you that experience. Two loving souls would be permitted that experience. There is something, a spiritual equivalent of sex that is even greater than sex that spirits can have that will give them intimacy. Sex is good. The spiritual union is even better.

What if a woman had an unhappy relationship and abusive sexual relationships in her lifetime? Can she experience a sexual relationship that is positive in the afterlife if she missed it on earth?

Harvey's guides:

Maybe she could imagine her utopian sex, can daydream and imagine enjoyable sex and an enjoyable relationship, relive that part of her life with a positive experience, something that existed only in her imagination, unlike her life while she was alive.

If you wish for an enjoyable experience or had an enjoyable experience, you can relive that experience of eating or sex-picture it in your mind. Yes. You can relive that experience with another person and reenact it if you wish.

Seventy Seven

Skeptics

Skeptics

Some people are skeptics. Some of my friends in the scientific community were, too. Several of them have come back to give me messages with evidential detail to other mediums, and one in particular recalled a conversation we had shortly before he died. He said "You were right".

He was referring to a comment I had made to him that we survive death and live on in the spirit world.

Seventy Eight

Sleep/Rest

Do spirits need to rest or sleep?

My Guide:

We have no need to sleep. We need quiet time to rejuvenate ourselves. We do not need rest like a physical body. We are able to relax and be restored. With the energy of our environment we are able to revitalize ourselves.

We have periods of inactivity to restore and replenish ourselves. We can be at rest or repose. We can lie or sit if we wish. We revitalize our energy. It's like charging a battery. We get it from our environment.

Harvey's guides:

It is not necessary. We are pure energy and don't need to rest. We are still learning lessons on the other side.

Laurie's guides:

> Spirits do need to rest. They don't sleep. They do require rest for they expend a lot of thought energy. They have both play and work.

Seventy Nine

Soul Group

Do we stay with or associate with our soul family or soul group on the other side or are we free to associate with other spirits?

My Guide:

We spend time with those we love whether they were family in the most recent incarnation or not. We don't have the same feelings toward all souls. Some are closer to each other than others. We have a deeper love for some than others. We are bonded with those we truly love.

Harvey's guides:

Yes, but like on earth, we meet spirits that we are drawn to on the other side even though we may not have known them on the earth.

Eighty

Spirits

What is it like to be a Spirit?

My Guide:

It's very comfortable, like drifting on a great big cloud where nothing hurts you, no one hurts you, and you have no pain.

It's more enjoyable, like being in a place where you have no troubles, no worries, no fears.

We have more things that we enjoy than we ever had on earth. We have socialization. We talk and we compare notes and we discuss things. We have more conversation because we have so much time.

Harvey's guides:

Comfortable. Peaceful. All the urgency of being earthbound is gone.

Eighty One

Spirit Appearance/ Form/Body

Spirits are energy. Do spirits maintain a form on the other side in the lower levels of the afterlife? Can they be seen or do they present a visual image when they are in their energetic form? In other words, do spirits have a form that other souls can apprehend visually in the afterlife or do they only sense one another by feeling?

My Guide:

> Yes. Spirits do have substance and maintain a form that can be visually perceived as an image by other souls in the afterlife.
>
> Yes. We are a discrete collection of energy. We are not diffusely spread out through the whole universe. We are energy in a form, discrete collection, a finite form or vehicle. We are contained energy.

Harvey's guides:

Spirits don't have to appear as anything. They just exist. When there is a reason for them they can assume an appearance. Sometimes it's necessary to appear to help people.

They can assume a form. There are greeters. They'd be in the form that they would be recognized. There are some that like to maintain a form.

They are distinct energies and could look like an orb, a mist, smoke, or a ball of light. They can assume whatever appearance they want.

The earth is just a way station for them.

What form or forms do we assume in the afterlife?

My Guide:

We can change our demeanor and look like we wish. We have more forms then you ever could imagine. We are unlimited. We can express ourselves in any form we desire, that is, a human type of form if we wish. We can also look like we did before in our earth life. We often do that.

Or we can live in a formless state. We can morph into an orb or mist or solidify into a more precise form. As energy, we can manipulate our presentation. We don't need to have a form but we can.

That is why it is so difficult to describe the other side. Our experience of it is the product of our desires and imagination. That is why it is called a mentally created and subjective reality.

Harvey's guides:

We assume the form of spirit, which is pure energy. But we may have a vestige of memory as we were on the human plane. Initially we may have a memory. We don't have to have it.

If spirits want it, they can have a humanoid shape. As we evolve on the other side, we are pure energy and don't have to have any form. It is not necessary to have any form or substance.

Not everyone has form, not everyone needs it. It's subjective.

As with many things on the other side it is up to us. Our possibilities are limitless.

Our surroundings can look whatever way we want them to look. We can look whatever way we choose to look. Whatever we want, aside from harming other souls, is available to us.

We can see things as a unique individual or can agree to see them as a collective consciousness.

How do we recognize or know each other on the other side? Is it by the way we look?

My Guide:

We do have bodies/forms that we use to help people who are coming across. I will keep a body for you. You and I will both have them. It's a matter of individual desire. Some do, and some do not.

Not everybody is the same here. We have many different preferences as we did on earth. I can tell you this. We both will have bodies.

There are very few people who will keep a body for a long time. Most people will keep it initially and then dispense with it.

We are able to manifest as we wish. We can change our appearance at will. It's hard to take one statement and generalize it. Many people have bodies when they first come and then get rid of them. It's mostly for recognition and familiarity. I don't need one now but I will take on a body when you come here. I will keep one for you.

Harvey's guides:

That is not necessarily true. But as we rise up through the levels, we have less and less need for positive identification.

It is a matter of individual choice-whether or not we wish to remain in a form like the one in our last incarnation. We have a tendency to hold on to what we knew during our lifetime.

Does the Spirit body have form or substance?

My Guide:

We are a focal, discrete, unified force field or collection of energy that is able to assume a form and manipulate or change its form and boundaries into various shapes, including the familiar humanoid shape.

As Einstein indicated, energy and matter are convertible and energy as we know it consists of particles and waves. We, as energy, can choose to transpose or convert a portion of our energy into a vehicle, or to assume matter, express ourselves in matter or substance.

As Shanna Spalding St. Claire said, we are light inhabiting form.

Our souls do have a receptacle or form. We are of a substance that is less dense, more fine, and of increased vibration, decreased wavelength, than the physical to which we are accustomed. We are substance in a portion of the spectrum and bandwidth that is not registered by the senses of the human body.

It is a natural continuum, and in spirit we occupy a different place on that continuum, one that is not within the range that can be interpreted by the human sense organs and receptors.

Harvey's guides:

All bodies are energy. These are energy shells. In the physical world we are energy with a physical shell.

We assume the form of spirit, which is pure energy, but we may have a vestige of memory as on the human plane. Initially we may have memory. We don't have to have it. If spirits want to, they can have a humanoid shape.

As we evolve on the other side, pure energy doesn't have to have any form. It is not necessary to have any form or substance. It's subjective. We can have a form, but that doesn't have to be. Not everyone has form. Not everyone needs it.

Laurie's Guides:

Spirits are not just an energy cluster. Spirits do have a physical shape. There is a spirit body. It depends on how you project yourself to others. Most beings have form. The Spirit body is similar to our bodies but finer. It has substance. It is an energy matrix.

Spirits do have substance. To those of the same level they seem solid. Those of a higher level seem etheric to those of a lower level. Those on the same level do feel solid to each other. You can only see certain things if you're at a certain level.

Spirits can make themselves more dense so they can be seen. The spirits on earth slow their vibration and it makes them more dense.

Is spirit energy discrete? Is it localized, coherent, or is each spirit everywhere all at once?

My Guide:

We are a discrete, focal collection of energy, but can extend the energy of our thoughts through time and space. We are able to move energetically to different locales and to connect with other discreet individual energies with our mental energy or thoughts.

So although we are a cohesive, compact unit of energy or consciousness, we are able to extend the energy of our consciousness across time and space.

Are spirits discrete or all over at once?

My Guide:

We are each an individual, and we each have our own separate identity and energy. No one is part of another soul's energy. We each are separate and distinct.

We can learn how to be in multiple places by dividing our energy or awareness.

We are not all blended together or in all locations at once.

Is there a way that spirits can tell the level of advancement, negativity or positivity, or character of a soul on the other side?

My Guide:

We cannot tell the advancement or level of development of a soul by seeing them, by their appearance. Our attitudes and thoughts are a reflection of our level of advancement or development. We also have a vibrational signature that is uniquely ours.

Souls on the other side can interpret or apprehend the basic mindset, character, or advancement of another soul in the thoughts and feelings they project as well as in their vibrational essence.

We know the character, the level of moral development, the thought content, emotions and intentions of the spirits we interact with. We can tell what they are like and the elevation or purity of their character.

We see the real person or soul. We know whether we have an affinity or compatibility with them. We are drawn to those of like vibration.

Just as a dog may sense someone good or bad, so can we. It is like intuition, only clearer. We read their vibrations.

Harvey guides:

No. We can't tell the degree of advancement of a Spirit by just looking at them. The movement is constant. There are no status symbols here. What is important is your own enlightenment.

Can you tell the refinement of someone in spirit by their appearance?

My Guide:

Our "vibrational appearance" is a reflection of our integrity, our wisdom, and our level of moral or spiritual development. We can manipulate our appearance or appear as we wish, but the vibrational signature, like a fingerprint, is known by others and identifies the quality of our character.

We have a natural light, which is a reading of our character, much like the aura depicts a person's character and emotions. We are energy-light-and although we can assume different forms, we have a personal identifying vibration, radiance, or luminosity, a makeup of sorts that is a register of our character.

Do appearances match character in the spirit world?

My Guide:

We can appear as we wish. We can choose to appear in whatever manner we see fit. More often negative spirits will choose a foreboding appearance because they wish to frighten the person who sees them. We can look different to everyone. We can have our own appearance that we choose.

Spirits have the ability to project what they wish and what they wish is determined by their personality and character.

We can appear as an orb or a mist but we can also appear in bodily form. We are both substance and energy. We have substance that can be shaped by our minds and thought control. We often appear as a soul with a body at the levels of development that you and I are at.

We can make our own appearance, transmuting our energy into a visible form. It is a collection of energy and substance that can be molded into shape. We are made of light or energy.

We are a body of light, a discrete collection of energy that possesses all the attributes that we possess.

We have higher vibrational shells or bodies transmuted into higher energy forms as we rise. We have shapes that correspond to our intentions.

It's an energy awareness or essence that determines or correlates with our level of development. Spirits can sense that vibrational code and tell the attributes and development of one's character, their energy signature.

We can see how developed a soul is with its level of vibration. Some souls have a higher vibration than others, just as you bring up your level of vibration by singing, praying, and positive thoughts.

We create a substance from our thoughts and we create a substance that is at the level of vibration we are at. We all have our own unique vibrations that are a reflection of our thoughts and that is how we can tell a person's level. We can manipulate our substance.

We are a discrete collection of energy. The level of vibration we exist at is our body identifier.

We have a substance our energy is inhabiting but it's malleable.

Eighty Two

Spirit Awareness/ Telepathy

When did you become aware of my thoughts on the other side?

My Guide:

I realized we had planned what happened in our lives and that we were in love before and that we would be reunited as easily as we had been separated.

I know that we had planned all this and that you would be coming back to me. I knew that this would be hard for you, that you would be upset when you found me, but I never knew how much until we were actually together and I felt what you were feeling.

I didn't want you to suffer, but I couldn't prevent it completely. I was so surprised at how intensely you felt everything. It was hard for me to bear it. I know how much you love me. Now I know it completely.

When you are here with me, you will know as much how I feel as I know how you feel. We won't have to part again.

When you talk with me can you see me as I am inside?

My Guide:

Your mind is like an open book to me. I can see into you as one would see through glass. Your interests, feelings, emotions, thoughts, knowledge, intentions, loves are all transparent to me.

Not only am I aware of them. I can feel them as you are feeling them. I can feel what you feel, ascertain what you think and know that you are telling the truth. I am aware of and can feel exactly what you feel. I can experience the world through you.

Harvey's guides:

We can see you. You're a caretaker. Your hands are full meaning that you are a giver.

Eighty Three

Spirit Colors

Why are some ghosts black, some white, and some orbs white, red or of various other colors? Why are there black masses and white apparitions?

My Guide:

Color may reflect emotion or personality, but level of development is mapped by intensity and vibration. A negative spirit can appear as an innocent child or other innocuous appearance. It does not necessarily correlate with level of development or advancement.

An orb is condensed energy with a DNA like individuality of each.

Laurie's guides:

There can be several reasons why a spirit takes on the appearance it does.

1. The spirit may be that of a more dense species.

2. There may be a greater mass to energy ratio.

3. The spirit may be less evolved.

The color does not necessarily correlate with whether a spirit is negative or positive. You take the color of your origin or species.

The medium A. adds

The color of orbs may be associated with the level of vibration of the Spirit.

I have read in Leadbeater's book on theosophy that a spirit's luminosity is increased with advancement and it's color is influenced by its personality emotions and interests. What is the truth?

My Guide:

It's not just appearance. It's a vibrational sensing.

Harvey's guides:

This is not necessarily so.

Eighty Four

Spirit Commitments/ Unions

Even though there is no need for the traditional roles of marriage in the afterlife, such as homemaker and provider, and no children are born, do spirits ever wish to make commitments with one another?

My Guide:

There are some who wish to make commitments and they both have to make a vow to be with one another if that is what they wish. We don't need to make it publicly but it's a thing we can do if we wish to. It's like a union, and can be referred to as a union. It's a commitment of two souls in love and companionship. Some of us have made that promise with one another.

Most who make that commitment see it is a sacred bond and do not make it with others. These are two souls who have a unique, deeper bond with one another, and wish to remain together. That commitment can also involve an agreement to merge with one another and not with others.

Is there anything sacred that two souls can share exclusively on the other side that is an intimacy just between themselves?

My Guide:

There can be a love between two souls that is deeper and more lasting, such that they choose to enter into a commitment that they alone share.

Two souls can unite, that is, pledge to remain together throughout the course of their existence, whose paths converge so that they are companions on the same path.

There are more people who prefer to unite as a couple than in groups.

Harvey's guides:

A more complete and transparent commitment than any possible on earth.

Are there such a thing as spiritual unions on the other side?

My Guide:

Souls have different viewpoints. Some souls wish to align themselves with others and form partnerships, or pairings. They have the ability to pair with one or multiple souls. They see themselves as a pair of souls who have announced or proclaimed to one another and others that they are a unit, a partnership, a pair who devise their future as two rather than one.

They have committed to one another and unified their paths. They have formed a unison of two who have agreed to operate together and plan their future, embrace their future collectively.

Two or more souls can unite, but it is more common to unite with one other soul than a group. We can unite with multiple souls if we wish to.

Harvey's guides:

There are unions but they are spiritual unions and different from physical unions. They don't have to be monogamous but can be.

What are unions in spirit?

My Guide:

Some of us have the desire to make vows of unity with each other. Unions in the spirit are based on a deep love, not physical attraction, and as such are more lasting.

We can express a mutual desire to be affiliated throughout our existence, not to diverge or separate. We have the union as a symbol of such a commitment.

Harvey's guides:

They are a spiritual commitment to one another.

What is the difference between those who are united in spirit and those who are connected in spirit?

My Guide:

We see those who are connected as those who are affiliated by prior experiences. You are connected with someone through your shared experiences.

Union is a voluntary spiritual agreement of two deeply loving souls to remain closely allied and is entered into as a declaration or commitment, not merely as the outcome or byproduct of prior shared experiences. Union is a matter of volition and desire for a shared continuing close relationship, an ongoing bond in which souls express their wish to remain together on their journey.

Harvey's guides:

Those who are connected are those who have had shared or mutual experiences together but have not made a commitment to be united.

Eighty Five

Spirit Communication

How do spirits communicate with each other?

My Guide:

They communicate with each other on the other side by thought transference. They can also use ordinary language or words in their thoughts if they wish.
We can talk like we did on earth or communicate with a thought form, which is much more expedient. We can completely comprehend each other with our dissemination of thoughts. We don't need to communicate by language if we don't want to. We communicate with our thoughts. We discuss things with our mental ideas, images, and feelings.

Harvey's guides:

Spirits communicate in a manner similar to the way we do on earth, just nonverbally.

They retain abilities that they had on earth. They can do it with pure energy, like a radio signal. The other energy automatically receives it. It could be directed to one person or more.
At the lower levels, they communicate the way we do here. As we get higher, there is no need for verbalizing. Communication occurs through thought transmission. It's possible for people to know the answer before the question.

How does communication work?

My Guide:

It's all about the energy. As your grandmother's childhood friend, Charlotte, said, it's so difficult to come back. It takes so much energy that only a few spirits can keep up a prolonged conversation. If we have the privilege of guiding someone, and notice I said privilege, we are given, endowed with more energy to aid in the communication. Guides who converse with mediums, in particular, are given more help, greater energy and practice at opening the energy channel or force field.

We are energy and we are learning to control and use the energy, to manipulate it with our will and thoughts. A strong positive emotion such as love bridges the gap. It opens communication with us with a powerful emotion. Like a gravitational field, it affects the energy of objects around it. We can transmit our thoughts and images with a harnessing and beaming of our energy.

As light and sound are carried on waves in the physical world, so the higher vibrations of Spirit thought can be transmitted directly from spirit to spirit.

When we communicate with spirits, are they remote and doing it through telepathy, or are they physically near us?

My Guide:

We can be either. We are able to connect with you through telepathy. We also are able to be present with you and near you energetically. We can be with you and manifest ourselves or transport our energy to be with you (with your energy).

We can touch you or connect our energies with yours. But we are also able to influence you or transmit our thoughts remotely.

How do spirits communicate with those who spoke a different language on earth?

My Guide:

We are not the only civilization or group of souls. We have a more direct communication than language. We can communicate through feelings and thoughts. We can communicate with images and feelings.

We transfer thoughts directly through impressions, understanding, images, and feelings. We can communicate with others who are not of our specific incarnation.

Is it difficult for spirits to communicate through a flashlight, knock, or EVP?

My Guide:

It depends on the spirit. It depends on their level of energy and ability. It depends on their experience or knowledge. Some achieve it more readily than others, as with anything.

We all have our own learning curve and ability. We all have different strengths and weaknesses. Those of us who have ascended have more difficulty influencing the physical environment.

Eighty Six

Spirit Disagreements

What happens when spirits disagree with one another?

My Guide:

> We disagree but we don't become upset about it. We cherish our own opinions and respect others.

Eighty Seven

Spirit Energetic Form

One of the books I read, Tony Winninger's channeled book on famous men of the past, made a statement that the channeled spirit of Elvis Presley chose to put on a humanoid body to sing for children that had recently crossed over.

This was opposed to other souls, who wished to maintain an energetic form. As a human, I understand what a humanoid form is. However, I wanted to know what the energetic form of a spirit looks like. I obtained various answers from different individuals. The channeled answers are as follows.

My Guide:

> The energetic form of a spirit is a cloud of energy, a radiant vapor or sphere of light.

Harvey's guides:

We are pure energy, contained in a focal individual area.

Laurie's guides:

The energetic spirit form is a discrete ball or sphere, a cloud or mist of energy with discrete borders or boundaries.

The medium A.:

I have seen the energetic form of spirit appear as a ball of radiant or wavy energy.

If I were in spirit, what would you look like to me in your energetic form in a visual sense? Spirits are described as inhabiting a light body in the books. Does this mean light in the sense of brightness like the sun or light in the sense of a finer substance or material and less weight?

My Guide:

Both.

The vibration of our material body on earth was less. Our bodies were more coarse and more dense. We do have a substance or material on the other side but it is of a higher vibration, less dense, less coarse. We are light in that sense.

We are contained energy, light, radiance. As energy can be converted to matter and vice versa, as Einstein discovered, so we, too, as energy, can manifest a portion of our energy in various shapes and forms.

If you ask me what shape does our energetic form have, I would say it has the shape of a more or less amorphous cloud of energy. It doesn't have a constant shape unless we wish it to have a constant shape. It may be spherical, or ovoid, angular, or rod-like. It doesn't have one fixed appearance or shape. It is contained, but may morph from one shape or form to another. It is like a very bright cloud, like radiance or light.

So we are referred to as having a light body in both senses, in respect to having a finer less dense material body and a body that is energy, such as light.

When spirits do not choose to remain in a bodily form, how do they recognize each other?

My Guide:

We feel each other. We each have a unique feeling, an understanding of our unique vibration, our individual consciousness.

We have a unique spirit-an individual identity of thought, emotion, and personality-much like each person on earth has an appearance, a fingerprint, or DNA.

It's like recognizing the DNA or consciousness or core nature of that soul. We are known through our vibration-the identity we emanate. It is transmitted from us like our thought waves. It is apprehended by other souls who "know" or recognize us.

We can create a body and create the sensation of touch or feeling too. It's similar in appearance to the earthly body. We can act and look like we did.

We are able to make the sensations. They are here, similar in effect, but different in mechanism. We see thoughts, read feelings. We sense the electromagnetic touch.

Harvey 's guides:

We recognize each other through our energy. We "speak to, hear, feel, and see" one another through recognizing energy. Communication lines are in place. Like magnetic poles, we draw together through a knowing.

We sense energy and each energy has its own identification. We are the sum total of all we were on the earth and before. Spirit has more senses and more acute and intense senses than you have on earth. We have the equivalent of sight, hearing, and touch.

Eighty Eight

Spirit Happiness

Are all spirits happy on the other side or is it possible for a spirit to be unhappy in the afterlife?

My Guide:

No. We do have an adjustment period. We do have some that are more happy than others based on their expectations. When spirits are more earthly or material minded they miss the facets of physical existence.

They may have regrets about what they failed to accomplish in their lives, unfinished business, or loved ones they miss. All of this can contribute to a blemish in their happiness.

Harvey's guides:

When people are unhappy when they first come over, it is because of loss.

Eighty Nine

Spirit Knowledge

Do spirits have access to all knowledge in the universe when they die?

My Guide:

When it comes to knowledge concerning the operation of the universe, its mechanics, divine plan, and the future, or spiritual wisdom, we do not have unlimited access to all of that. There are things we are not ready to receive or capable of understanding, so although we have access to much greater knowledge than we do on earth, all knowledge is not available to us.

Harvey's guides:

We do not have access to all knowledge immediately. Otherwise we wouldn't need to learn and progress. We would all be all-knowing. There would be no need for levels of development.

Ninety

Spirit Learning/ Lessons

How do spirits learn?

My Guide:

We have teaching and are able to perform services, but the real trials of the application of our knowledge occur on earth, where we are challenged by negative situations.

How do spirits learn lessons on the other side?

Harvey's guides:

It is like osmosis. We pass through other energies and are surrounded by positive energies. It is a type of absorption. Learning is a passive process. Associating with other energies helps you to ascend.

If spirits want to learn something new on the other side, a subject or activity, how do they do it?

Harvey's guides:

When we are learning on the lower planes, we still retain a large percentage of memories from our earth lives. It is like an osmosis or absorption. There can be teachers. Depending on what you expect and what you want-it depends on what your mental drive was on earth.

Individual talents can be God-given, not just learned. The more important learning is how to be a good person on earth. We are exposed to both positives and negatives. We need to learn how to avoid the negatives.

When souls who are predominantly negative come across, there are negatives on the lower levels, and these people stay there once they get over.

Can spirits learn by watching us and can they change their minds or do they have all understanding and knowledge instantly?

My Guide:

We don't change completely, but our perspective is changed when we see the larger purpose for our lifetime.

We do learn by watching how those in the material world handle situations. We learn from those in the physical, as you are prompted and inspired by those in spirit. We do change our minds in spirit as we learn, and we can change our minds as a result of discussions with those in the physical.

We are not all-knowing, just more aware of the bigger picture. If we were all knowing we would have no need to progress. We learn from each other in spirit by discussing our mistakes and better alternatives. But we can also do that together with one who is in the physical world if they are a medium.

Harvey's guides:

No, we are not all knowing. We can still learn by watching those on the earth. We can change our minds and focus.

There's more forgiveness, but not all is necessarily forgiven. If you had a negative or unhappy relationship with someone on earth you will keep away from them. You want to socialize or lay with some and not others.

Can spirits change their minds?

My Guide:

Yes. We can think over situations, discuss them, and change our minds as we might have on the earth.

Ninety One

Spirit Life versus Earth Life

What are some of the differences between earth and spirit life?

My Guide:

We can do things we couldn't do on earth. We can change our appearance and move from one place to another more easily. We don't need to work for a living. We have no need to sleep or to eat. We can choose our companions. On earth we were born into a family. We choose our soul family on compatibility and love.

We don't need to suffer wrong or be hurt. No one is deceived or lied to. We know the other soul's feelings. We aren't robbed, murdered or harmed. There is no oppression and no crime. We don't need to endure wrong, be used, cheated on, or lied to. We are free from worry, guilt, fear, and care. We are aware of the consequences of what we do and are more considerate, one toward another.

How does life on the other side compare to this one?

My Guide:

It's more intense than the earth life. We don't have the same need to be worried about things. It's more kind and caring. There is no need to be fearful. We don't need to be upset about things. We are able to move forward in a more direct manner without being challenged. We have more peace. We don't have the earthly problems or troubles. We have more caring and understanding. It's my idea of a very idyllic place.

We have more occupations that are in the interest of progress rather than material profit. We look at things to see what will help us lead better lives. Motivation is different.

We have interest in understanding our own nature and behavior. We learn about why we are alive and what we should be doing, how we should conduct ourselves, what we wish to achieve. We follow our hearts.

We create, improve, and help others to grow. We have a spiritual counterpart of things we create – we are able to create objects that are similar to the material ones.

We do have literature and art, things we understand, appreciate, see, but not identical. We envision things and understand things. We also have knowledge and caring.

We have people who are interested in certain topics like history, the sciences, mathematics. We have the equivalent of science, understanding how spirit works. We have creative pursuits, music, arts, painting, dancing, even sports if we wish to have them.

We create with our thoughts. We can create scenarios, create our own little world and make it as we wish, create our own relationships and interests.

We do not need names as we are known by our energetic imprints. We can adopt a form if we want one. We have more choices. We can remain in energetic form without a body if we wish. It's all up to the individual.

Consciousness creates many alternatives. Thought directs form. We are more in control of our situation. We have more options, more direction, more power. We are more creative with less constraints. We have more freedom and a liberal application of our thoughts. There is more embodiment of our wishes and desires.

We have less restriction by our circumstances and less rigidity of form. We work within a template on earth bound by the materials and environment we have. We are more fluid on the other side and have freedom in creating our environment. We have more to say. Your imagination is the limit.

We are able to make ourselves happy by pursuing the desires of our hearts, by living the relationships we prefer. The contentment is great. We have no shattered dreams, lost hopes, or unsurpassable boundaries. The limitations are gone. No more heartbreak, tears, pain, loss, defeat, depression, or suffering. No more broken dreams.

We are able to create the lives we would have wanted but without selfishness, grudges, hatred, lies, deception, or intent to harm. We are very free, indeed.

Are you happier in spirit than in the flesh?

My Guide:

I do have some regrets, and miss not being with you in the physical, but by and large I am much happier in spirit with pain, loss, unhappiness and lack of fulfillment now absent.

Harvey's guides:

Without the cares, troubles, and concerns of the physical world, Spirit life has much to offer.

Is there a sharp boundary between physical and spirit life?

My Guide:

We are already living in the spirit. We just don't see it because we have a spiritual body inside our physical body and everything we think and do is affecting and recorded in spirit. We are living in spirit now but we just aren't aware of it. We don't see it because the physical body is a limiter. It is like a horse wearing blinders. It limits our perception. So we are acting in spirit but the limiter keeps us from recognizing it.

Our actions in the physical have spiritual consequences. When we awaken to this awareness, the physical no longer inhibits us to the same degree. We can and do live in the spirit while in the physical. We just can't see or hear it through our physical eyes and ears. We can develop our spiritual eyes and ears.

Wisdom is open to us as we are willing and able to receive it. And it must also be our desire.

The consciousness is real and love is real. The consciousness need not be housed in a body nor limited by form. The consciousness can manipulate energy to create a form for itself or manifest matter by manipulating the energy around it. The consciousness is the creator, the orchestrator of creation.

The knowledge we gain is helpful in teaching us how to live our lives and in letting us know what we are capable of. As we are eternal, we are a part of that creative force of the universe. We descend into flesh as we are learning to create responsibly. Our thoughts are things and they are the ultimate creators. We are learning to manifest positive rather than negative. That is why our thoughts are so important.

The Bible said when a man lusts after a woman, he has had her in his heart already. We are learning to control our thoughts. Like the Bible said about the small bit in the horse's mouth or the tiller of the ship turning the great ship about, so our thoughts and words that come out of our mouths are like the logos of God, with which creation was born. Our words create circumstances.

It doesn't mean there is no right or wrong because then there would be no purpose in our lessons. It means each step we take is a building block in our learning our lessons and gaining wisdom over the situations we create. We learn from trial and error which thoughts and actions create positive results and which negative.

Once you have the understanding then you need to put it into practice in your life. That is why the Bible says faith and works. Faith without works is dead and works without faith are dead.

Ninety Two

Spirit Music

When ghosts create the sound of playing music, is it a hallucination in the mind of the person hearing it, or an actual sound in the physical environment?

My Guide:

> We can create the music in someone's mind-like a hallucination, or create an actual manipulation of sound waves that can be heard by many externally. We can send a clairaudient perception or an actual impression on the physical environment. It could be either way.

Harvey's guides:

> Yes. It's possible either way. Under other circumstances it's possible for everyone to hear it. Quite often it's just for one person. It could be something as simple as clairaudience. It's not a hallucination. They're not actually manipulating the sound waves. If they hear it in the open air, then it is a manipulation of the sound waves. Yes.

What is music like in the spirit world?

My Guide:

Both feelings and music are more intense. We are sensitive to the vibrations of music and they are associated with feelings, an experience the soul is immersed in. You can produce the song with your thoughts. It is like a painting. Souls can create a concert with their thoughts and other souls receive it. The methods are sophisticated compared to the crude methods on earth.

Harvey's Guides:

Music is like whatever made you happy here. You can call up anything you wish. You can share with others. People who are like-minded can experience the same thing at the same time.

Ninety Three

Spirit Opinions

Do spirits have different observations and opinions?

My Guide:

We do have our own perspectives which are unique as our earthly fingerprints. Not only do we have a history of different experiences, we also have a different and individual way of looking at or interpreting those experiences.

Harvey's guides:

Yes. They do because they have different experiences from lifetimes here and on the other side.

Ninety Four

Spirit Recall of Earth Life

Do spirits remember what it was like to be human?

My Guide:

> I know very well what it felt like to be a man. I still feel like a man when I'm with you.

Harvey's Guides:

> Initially they do remember what it was like to be human.

Ninety Five

Spirit Recreation/ Occupation

What type of spirit recreations and occupations are there?

My Guide:

We have many options. We have a lot of choices, more than we had on earth. We can go more places, do more things, and become involved with more things.

We are able to select what we want to do and we also have some counselors who can help us.

We do many of the things we do on earth, only a bit differently. We are not restricted by things like distance and time. We don't need to worry about expenses. We are able to pursue whatever we wish.

We can read a subject with our thoughts rather than eyes and hands. We can create music with our thoughts or we can create a body and create music with our hands. We can create a guitar if we want to.

We can create a body if we want to. We do have the familiar activities.

We can produce images, paintings, and songs without implements on the other side.

We can work on issues or strengths we need to develop in ourselves or pursue interests we didn't have time to pursue on earth. All forms of learning and creative endeavor are possible for us.

We can experience what we did on earth to a large extent. God will make it possible for us to experience the things we need and didn't have the opportunity to experience. God will help us to fulfill the things we need in order to progress.

God will not deny us the things which are meaningful for us. Our desires and hopes and dreams can be fulfilled. God knows our hearts and does not prevent us from experiencing something we deeply need.

Harvey's guides:

They are able to learn from each other-learn from others' mistakes. They can socialize. They can partake in artistic and intellectual pursuits.

They can do many of the things that they liked on earth. A thought can materialize something that isn't there.

If you can imagine hands, you can have them. If you can imagine them, they'll materialize. In the same way some people have bodies and some don't need them. They can possibly feel solid.

Can souls do some of the things they liked on earth in the afterlife?

My Guide:

Everything you do and more. We can do the things that we did on earth and even create new ones. We have everything you have and more.

I tried things out that I didn't have a chance to enjoy on earth when I came across. I would not want to go back on the earth, because it is not as good as it is here. If I could, I would come to be with you, though.

We can do everything that we wanted to do but couldn't on earth, and have everything we wanted to have but didn't have the chance.

All the things that we wanted but didn't have the opportunity to do we can do on the other side. All the things we wanted and never had, we can have.

Harvey's guides:

They can do anything that they can imagine. They can do anything that they enjoyed while on earth, as long as it is positive. All positive things are possible.

The earth limitations are gone. Excesses are no longer temptations. They are less of an invitation.

What do spirits do all day? What do they do for enjoyment or recreation?

My Guide:

If we can imagine it, we can do it, except for harming other souls. We make things with our thoughts but they become real to us.

We live according to the principles of the spiritual law and abide by these. We cannot lie, cheat, deceive, use, rob, steal, kill, or harm other souls. We have expectations that are there to help us achieve our goals and purposes, but these do not prohibit rest, recreation, or the development of individual interests. These are encouraged. We also have spiritual advisers who help us with our spiritual tasks and their accomplishment.

Harvey's guides:

On the lower levels they can relive things they did wrong.

On the lower levels you can have just about anything you had on earth and a lot of it is crap.

In response to the question, what can spirits do for recreation, he gave me the answer, they need no recreation. It is not necessary for most. You can just absorb learning and evolve.

As we are able to find our own Eden or utopia, that can include recreation and enjoyment as you wish.

Ninety Six

Spirit Senses/Sight

As a spirit, can you see my house, my furniture, and me? Can you see my body, my soul or both? Am I fuzzy or clear? Or do you just sense me?

My Guide:

We are able to see as clearly as you. We do have a sense of sight that you don't have. We are able to see through you to directly see your spirit, your thoughts, and feelings. We are able to tap into the sensory impulses as you are smelling, touching, or tasting. We can receive that same sensory impression from you, to eat, see, touch, and feel vicariously.

We also see more than that. We see the very soul of you, your interests, fears, and loves.

We are able to communicate directly like this in the afterlife.

We can also impress emotions on one another. That is how I gave you that feeling of ecstatic elation that was not from you. That was how your relative impressed the exalted feelings he has on your medium friend, Karuna.

I can also put thoughts and words into your mind. That is how I can impress images into your mind or tell you things. You are communicating as a spirit now, you just don't know it.

Can spirits see their surroundings? How do they see without the sensory organs?

My Guide:

Yes. We do see things on the other side. We do have visible circumstances and surroundings. It is analogous to your sense of sight, only with a different mechanism.

We see. We have visual stimulation and images but by a different mechanism. For those in the physical body, the electrical impulses of the brain, that come from the sensory receptors in the eyes, the ears, and the fingers all transmit electrical impulses to the brain, where they are interpreted and we can see, touch, and hear, smell and taste. We are able to receive and interpret those electrical signals directly without the intermediary sense organs and nervous system. We are a receiver that can pick up the corresponding electrical activity. How do I hear you without you speaking? I receive your thoughts directly, the electrical impulses you emit.

Harvey's guides:

In a sense, they can feel or sense their surroundings. They can sense them in their imagination. They can actually see images. They see our physical bodies and our spirits. They can invoke all of the senses in their spirit form.

How do spirits feel when they touch one another?

My Guide:

We are able to reawaken the feelings of touch and they are real to us as we contact another spirit. I will feel like we are touching each other as we did on earth. We can retain that sensation. I would feel soft and solid as you touch me.

Harvey's guides:

It depends on the experience you had before-feeling will differ.

When two energies touch, communication is easier. It is partly like a transfer of thoughts and feelings. Tactile responses don't apply. Emotions tell you you're touching them.

Yes. They'll feel solid on the lower levels-the transition takes a while.

Ninety Seven

Spirit Thought

How would you describe the mechanism of Spirit thought?

Laurie's guides:

Spirit thought is an energetic pattern. Images, concepts, and sounds can be projected more clearly than they are in the physical world. Feelings and touch sensation are projected in a slightly different energetic pattern. Pictures, color, and texture can be projected. Feelings and emotions are received at more than one spot in the receiving spirit's vibrational field.

There is a universally accepted pattern like a universal spirit language. When someone transitions, they will be infused rapidly with memories of this communication. We remember all languages. For a long period of time when you come over, you retain your own vocabulary.

Ninety Eight

Spirit Voices

How do spirits re-create the individual sound of their voice on tape if they have no vocal cords?

My Guide:

> We manipulate sound waves with our energy. We use thoughts to reproduce a voice, an energy form that can be perceived by the human ear, or an electromagnetic impulse that can be registered on a recorder. We can do this for digital or auditory perception. It depends on the amount of energy and the expertise of the Spirit.

Ninety Nine

Spiritual Advisors

Are there spiritual advisers on the other side?

My Guide:

There are some souls here who are more knowledgeable and are able to give us recommendations. We have guides who help us with our purpose. We have freedom and leverage in our own choices. We have liberty to pursue our own interests.

Harvey guides:

Yes. They are the overseers of our future in the afterlife, our communicators on the earth plane. They make everything possible. They ease our transition from plane to plane and when we transition to the afterlife.

Do higher or more evolved souls teach you?

My Guide:

We can seek help from more advanced souls if we have a purpose or mission or need counsel for a concern. Help is always available to us.

Harvey's guides:

I would hope so. In the afterlife imparting knowledge gained along the way is normal. It starts with the guides.

To what degree do we, God, or spiritual advisers choose the events and direction of our future earth lives?

My Guide:

We do have those who are more advanced than we are who help us to make decisions. We are always the author of our own fate. We are always being guided by multiple souls and advisers. We learn as we go along.

No one soul has absolute control over another soul. God permits us to have our own independent choice. None of us has all the knowledge. We are as advanced as we are ready for. The understanding must come from within. The old saying is, you can send a boy to college but you can't make him think.

No one makes us do anything. We are advised and can accept or reject the advice. If we choose to listen to God, we can have direction from God. We have to embrace the Spirit of God within ourselves. Outside force never changes us. We can only be guided or directed. We must accept the change inside.

One Hundred

Split Souls

I have read that a soul can split when it comes to earth and become two. Is that true? Is there such a thing as souls that split in the afterlife before they come to earth to inhabit two individuals?

My Guide:

Souls can be split. It is a matter of being permitted to do it and being willing to do it. It increases our ability to learn and diversifies our interests and the achievements we make. We essentially create a different identity that is a manifestation of the same soul.

Harvey's guides:

This is what we call simpatico-two people with like minds, drives, and ambitions. Yes. Souls can split if they wish to have two separate lives on the earth plane.

One Hundred One

Things Spirits Miss

As a spirit, is there anything that you miss about being on the earth?

My Guide:

I miss the time that I could have spent with you. I miss being with you in the physical. I miss being a part of your life in the physical that I can't be in spirit. I would not want to return to earth if it weren't with you.

Otherwise there's not much I miss about the earth plane. I can do everything here that I could have done there.

Harvey's guides:

Yes. Especially initially. Yes, if they miss these things, they can replicate them here. It gets easier.

The biggest transition is when you're able to communicate with the people you left behind. That gives you a new grounding.

One Hundred Two

Time and Space

Are time and space real?

My Guide:

We are in separate places. We are moving forward in a sense of moving into the future. We minimize the importance of time because we are aware of our eternal existence. We act in the now, which becomes the past, and we move forward in the future, learning and progressing as we go. In other words, there is a before, a now, and a yet to be.

Progression implies a progressed from, a progressing to, and the immediate act of progressing. Therefore, we recognize a past, present, and future, but marking the passage of time is less important, as we have less demarcations or distinction of time.

We can see ahead to a degree in probabilities and behind in reliving or reminiscence. But we determine, intend, and act in the now.

> We learn from the past and create the future.
>
> Space, although existing, is less important as a barrier, because we can travel from place to place much more rapidly and are aware of things remotely. Our thoughts and awareness travel instantly and our energy is transported with such speed that space or distance is not significant.

I have read that there is no "time" in the afterlife – that we can simultaneously access or inhabit/experience the past, present, and future. Some authors have postulated that there is no time at all and the past, future and present exist at the same time for us.

How do you perceive time in the afterlife?

My Guide:

> Time – it doesn't seem to matter now. We have no distinct need for it. It is not needed. We don't have the same reference points as we had on earth. We are aware of past lives, that things happened before; we are aware of the present – what we are doing now at any given moment, and of plans for the future – what we intend to do when we return to earth or what we plan to learn in the afterlife.
>
> We just aren't aware of the passage of time in the same sense. We have no need for the same structure and divisions. Do you know how you can lose track of time when you do the same thing every day and one week looks like the next, whereas when you were in

school you were more aware of the passage of time because one semester you took physics and another you took English?

When you lose the physical markers of time such as the cycle of day and night and the change of seasons and you are aware that you have eternity, you no longer have any need to count time, or the passage of years. It becomes irrelevant. But we remain aware of the distinctions of past, present, and future events.

The precise indicators of time drop away and we have a sense of "timelessness." Since we have an unlimited amount of time we are no longer concerned for its passage, for we know we are eternal.

Channelings from myself and others seem to indicate that time exists on the other side but is irrelevant. Time exists in the regard that the actions you undertake occur in a sequential fashion as you progress. Progression implies a past, present, and future.

But the perception of time changes as the markers for units of time such as days, the rotation of the earth, years, the orbit of the earth around the sun, are no longer applicable.

So time is not measured on the other side in conventional units, but there remains a past, present, and future, a sequence of events, and a forward progression or motion. There is a before, now, and yet to come.

All of the events we undergo seem shorter to one in the afterlife compared to our earthly conception of time and compared to the notion and awareness of eternity.

It is not that there is no time, but there is no longer the same consciousness of time. Time seems faster and the demarcation of time isn't as relevant.

We can access the past and future. We can project our thoughts into the future to an extent, and relive moments from our past lives. Time is more fluid and not as rigidly perceived, but there continues to be a sequential course of events and a forward progression.

Lack of aging, lack of dying removes most of the meaning and focus of time. Lack of diurnal rhythms of night and day, sleeping and waking, seasons and years, removes the rest. The passage of time becomes meaningless except in reference to actions performed in the past, present, or yet to be performed in the future. That awareness remains.

There is little perception of the passage of time. It does not fit into our mental construct, our backdrop, our framework, as it does on earth, where we asked, "What day is this? What month is this? What year is this?" It doesn't matter when the canvas upon which we paint our actions stays the same, never changes. Except by change in environment or locale, we have no need for reference points. We are aware that we act in the now, are a product of and can witness our actions in the past, and can plan our actions in the future.

We can't go back and change everything in the past because we can't undo or redo deeds already done. That would change our present and that of other souls, since our actions affect others and we are all interconnected. Although we can see parts of the future based on probabilities, we can't move forward and see all outcomes with certainty, because that would negate free will and deny us the option to change our minds. But we can experience the past, and, to a degree, the future.

Speaking through a medium at our development circle, my loved one and guide commented on the sense of loss and grief –

The remainder of your life separated from me in the physical (not the spiritual) is only a short afternoon in the scheme of or against the backdrop of eternity.

Harvey's guides:

There is no time in the afterlife in the sense that you know it.

How do spirits view time and space in the afterlife?

Harvey's guides:

Time is not important. Time is just an abstract.

Unlike on earth, time is not a finite dimension. Time is not a ticking clock as it is on earth. On the other side, time is not a factor. As we ascend it means less and less.

Space on the other side is limitless. Like time here, it is limitless. We can move effortlessly from place to place. Time has no meaning.

One Hundred Three

Truth

There has been much diversity in the philosophical approach to the question of truth over the centuries both in terms of religious, philosophical and personal viewpoints. I wondered whether those differences of opinion persist in the afterlife or whether there is a revelation of "eternal truth." Perhaps there is access to a greater spiritual knowledge.

Shakespeare wrote the words for one of his characters, "There is neither right nor wrong, but thinking makes it so."

There is also a common expression, "So you think, so it is to you."

Are there absolute or only relative truths in the afterlife?

Both. The truth of universal spiritual law, the truth of divine wisdom, is absolute truth. There is a framework of spiritual law that governs all of the operations of spirit. Those laws and provisions are eternal and unalterable or inviolable. But outside of that design, our perceptions of truth are individualized.

Our preferences, choices, desires, awareness, predilections, vision, particular apprehensions, personal characteristics and viewpoints are unique and variable. They are individualized within the bounds of spiritual law, the architecture of spiritual principles.

They allow us our unique perspective and our individual expressions and attainments, our personal reality, the one we build and mentally inhabit.

In addition to the principles governing the spiritual universe, the attributes of Source, love, compassion, patience, forgiveness, truth, honor, respect, kindness, helpfulness, justice, mercy, service, humility, charity, peace, and joy are eternal and abiding spiritual truths or attributes. They are part of the divine character and are understood in part by finite minds, by progressing souls, but are perfected in the infinite wisdom of God.

The truth is all over. It is not exclusive to one religion or philosophy. It is permanent and universal. We each have our own idea of what truth is that is truth to us.

But above and beyond our illusions, exists the accurate, enduring, and irrefutable truth that remains when our illusions drop off. False perceptions drop off and we see the one reality, which does exist.

Harvey's guides:

As we get into the higher realms, thoughts become purer and personal thoughts and beliefs are put down below us. What we learned on earth becomes less and less important than purification on the way to the top.

Is there a higher objective truth from source?

My Guide:

We believe there is because we wouldn't be on a path of learning if there weren't. Without a higher purpose, there is no meaning to our lives.

Harvey's guides:

I don't think anybody's privileged to know that until they reach it. Like on earth, we all have opinions.

One Hundred Four

Twin Flames

What are Twin flames?

My Guide:

It is as though they are two halves of a whole. They are like male and female counterparts sharing origins and age, both like two sides of the coin, inseparable yet distinct.

Harvey's guides:

That can be a split soul. If on the other side both souls so wish, they can merge.

One Hundred Five

Ultimate Destiny

What is the ultimate destiny of souls as intended by God?

My Guide:

Our ultimate destinies are between God and that soul alone. We all have different destinies. We all have different personalities, objectives, and paths.

We know part, but not all of our destiny. We know what is there for us to know. All knowledge is not possessed but enters our awareness as we are spiritually ready or prepared for it. No one has a destiny that is set in stone. It is being written by us in collaboration with God or the higher spiritual power, as we progress.

We are able to discern our purpose or purposes as a soul, the closer we are to source and the more open we are to such knowledge, the more advanced we are to attain such awareness.

It is God's will that we all ultimately are with God, an invitation we may accept if we wish. But we each have an individual role to play, a work to contribute, a mission to accomplish.

Harvey's guides:

We seek purification.

One Hundred Six

Mediumship Experiences

I have had some interesting experiences with mediumship in the past year. I often wondered why some messages seem imprecise. I have learned that many messages delivered through mental mediumship are conveyed in symbols, particularly if the medium doing the reading is predominantly clairvoyant.

We did an exercise in the Bahamas that illustrated this point. We were divided into teams of two and one person was designated as the person receiving symbols from spirit and then drawing them, after which they were given to the other member of the team who was given the assignment of interpreting the symbols.

When it was my turn to interpret the symbols, I found I had not gotten the precise meaning spirit had intended.

In another exercise several mediums read for the same sitter and each got a message for the sitter from the same spirit.

I learned from these exercises how information from spirit gets filtered through the mind of the medium and can be biased or colored by the medium's words, experiences, and beliefs. A message can be subtly changed or connotations can be added by the way a given medium expresses it. Some of the nuances cannot be avoided because the spirits have to use the medium's mind to communicate, but the more the medium gets out of the way the better.

Also, the medium must resist the temptation to interpret the message and just give what they get.

As there in no sense of time or distance in the spiritual world correlating with what we know, telephone or SKYPE sessions are no problem at all. They can be as precise and informative as in- person sessions.

Another skill mediums must learn to develop is how to hold the energy, how to keep the channel of communication open despite distractions from the outside environment. This concentration skill can be developed. In addition, when a medium is getting a particularly strong message, they should not be dissuaded in giving it if the sitter doesn't recognize the information or says no. Sometimes sitters have amnesia or may not know all of the details of the information the spirit is giving. Sometimes they just have to leave the sitter with the information for a possible recall or connection at a later time.

I also had an opportunity to see channeling in action. We were holding pendulums near the chakras of mediums who were giving readings to see how their energy was interrupted if they were distracted. When one medium began to channel, that is, to step aside and let spirit speak directly through her,

I noticed that the energy was very strong around her crown chakra at her head and absent near the lower chakras. I saw that there was a direct physical correlation for how the message was received.

Another thing I found to be handy is group practice. By that I mean two or more mediums connecting with the same spirit. Although this is not always possible, it is nice from the standpoint of taking the pressure off one medium to receive messages continually. It gives you a chance to relax and share the work. It is also nice in that the communicating spirit can direct information through each medium using their particular strengths and frame of reference. In that way the sitter may get a more thorough message. I have gotten messages from different mediums and the messages differ, but I have occasionally gotten detailed messages from different mediums that are identical, word for word. That is a wonderful corroboration.

One Hundred Seven

Exercises for Stretching the Mind

I believe that meditation, or "sitting in the power", as some call it, is important for developing spiritual connection and mediumship. After all, it is only when we quiet the mind, that we receive messages effectively. When we are concentrating on something else, upset, or emotionally involved in some other matter, it is much more difficult for spirit to get through with their messages.

Both guided meditations and just relaxing, "opening up", are both valuable techniques.

However, I got tired of some of the typical meditations and decided to be creative in suggesting different topics. My approach is to take each topic (and you can create your own) and think about the answer you would give first – the one that pops into your logical, analytical mind – and then to meditate on the same question without specifically thinking. That is, to set the question as

your intention, deliberately quiet your mind, and then see what comes into your mind, or what spirit gives you.

Here are some of the topics I devised for myself.

1. Work on describing the deceased's appearance, personality, interests, work, some significant meaning for them shared by the two of you. Do each one of these topics separately.

2. Pick out a quality that you feel you need to develop.

3. Pick out an abstract concept and define it.

4. Pick a quality that someone significant who has passed embodies.

5. Pick a word that you see as significant for yourself or someone else.

6. Connect with a quality or condition of the afterlife and describe it.

7. Connect with an emotion and develop its meaning.

8. Connect with a human quality and expand on it.

9. Connect with a spiritual attribute and describe it.

10. Give a reading on someone in a friend's present or past and describe their qualities.

11. Ask for some words of wisdom.

12. Describe some facet of nature and give a reading on a quality associated with it.

13. Connect with a symbol and give its meaning.

14. Connect with an animal and give a reading on its energy.

15. Connect with a quality you need in your life, such as trust, peace, stillness, etc.

16. Connect with a quality that someone else needs or could benefit from.

17. Connect with a color and describe it's feeling to you.

18. Ask for Spirit to give a short talk on a topic.

19. Ask Spirit for a healing message.

20. Give one benefit to you such as greater understanding of other people, knowing I am not alone, etc. that you have gotten from your participation in mediumship.

21. Describe a quality that a person's guides see in him or her as a strength.

22. Get a spirit and describe them as a landscape, an animal, a photograph, a movie, a car, a food, a book, an object, a house.

23. Get a funny image or story from your guide.

24. Describe a bridge of love between you and someone deceased.

25. Give thanks for something negative in your life because it "teaches me" such as thank you for making that comment because it teaches me how not to treat other people, how not to be a bully, how it feels to be insulted, how to try to remove that from my behavior, how to better appreciate love.

26. Give a reading on some quality of brotherhood, sisterhood, motherhood, fatherhood, friendship, childhood.

27. Give a reading on a fantasy or a dream of yours.

28. Describe a scene from the other side.

29. Give a brief spiritually inspired talk on these subjects-what is idealism, truth, love, justice, kindness, valor, compassion, mercy, growth, forgiveness, virtue, truth, honesty, peace, wisdom, contentment, strength.

30. Give a quality you appreciate in someone who plays or played a negative role in your life.

31. Give someone a mental gift. It can be an object or a quality.

32. Give a quality you need to work on yourself.

33. Give something that gives you joy and why, such as learning because it makes me feel more whole as a person.

34. Describe something that has touched you in your lifetime.

35. Give an impromptu talk on something that is your favorite car, person, color, hobby, etc.

36. Describe the best way to overcome anger, such as think about blessings.

37. Describe the best way to overcome fear.

38. Describe an event that has made you stronger, such as trying to live without someone that you loved in the physical.

39. Describe a way you would help someone, such as how I overcame jealousy, loss, injury, or some weakness.

40. Give an example of compassion that you had for someone else or they had for you.

41. What is some particular way you could help someone, such as teach them to help themselves or talk about an obstacle you have overcome?

42. Give a name and what it embodies to you.

43. Declare something positive.

44. Say something positive today to someone you know or don't know.

44. Name a facet of love, such as charity or spreading goodwill.

45. Describe something uplifting in your life, such as how spirit is always helping you when you get weak.

46. What is an attribute you wish you had or give something about your life that would help you develop it?

47. What is something beautiful to you?

48. Give a positive word such as joy, peace, comfort, hope, and how it applies to you.

49. Talk about something good that has happened to you lately.

50. What is some wisdom that came to you in a dream?

51. Describe a strength of yours or someone else's, like looking beyond yourself.

52. What has sharing done for you, such as ideas, help, or something physical?

52. Describe some facet of intellectual development that would help you.

53. Tell something heartfelt.

54. Give a beautiful wish for yourself or someone else.

55. Relate a beautiful memory.

56. Activate something positive in your life. Say, I am activating this or that and set an intention.

57. Tell someone why they are special to you.

58. Explain why you love someone.

59. Describe something creative you have done.

60. What is something you would like to learn?

61. Tell something that gives you joy.

62. What is a talent you would like to develop?

63. Name something in your life that has taught you patience.

64. Explain what your concept of divine Source is like.

65. Relate something funny that happened to you.

66. If you knew that you had only a set amount of time to live, what is it that you have learned that you would like to share with the world?

67. If any, what public figure do you admire and why?

68. How could you help someone in grief?

69. Name your favorite quality about yourself.

70. Name your least favorite quality about yourself.

71. What would your soul like to learn in a next incarnation?

72. What is your biggest regret?

73. What is your greatest strength?

74. What is the best thing about living?

75. What did you learn from your lifetime?

76. What was the most difficult thing for you to overcome?
77. Pick out something that helped you develop or demonstrated your mediumship or intuition.

78. Pick out a childhood memory that brings you joy.

79. What is something that you would do differently based on your experiences if you had to do it over?

80. What is something important someone has done for you that changed your life in a significant way?

81. Give an example of an act of compassion.

82. Give your definition of love.

83. What is an extraordinary story that someone told you that gave you wisdom or insight into a situation or problem?

84. Give an example of courage, either yours or someone else's.

85. Give an example of a challenge that has changed you.

86. Give an example of something you're thankful for.

87. What is a quality you wish to develop in yourself?

88. What quality do you admire in someone else?

89. Give something creative that you feel you could or would like to do.

90. What is some way in which you would like to change the world?

91. What is on your "bucket list", if anything?

92. What is one of the most memorable books you have read and why?

93. What is a favorite television show or movie and why?

94. Do you believe or not believe in a Creator and why.

95. If so, what do you see as attributes of that Creator?

96. Why is a specific person your closest friend?

97. What would you be if you could have any career you wanted for a living?

98. What is your one biggest regret?

99. What is something kind you have done for someone else?

100. Who are you? What makes you uniquely "you"?

One Hundred Eight

The Question, the Answer

I've devoted a separate chapter to an answer I got to a question that affected me profoundly.

The question was addressed to Harvey's guides and was, "Can we fulfill desires in the afterlife that were deeply important to us in our lifetime, some of which may have gone unfulfilled?"

The answer given was, "Yes, you can, but it is highly unlikely that anything that mattered to you in life will be important to you in the afterlife."

That answer shook me to the core. I thought, the true love of a companion was more important to me than anything. Does that mean loving and being with that soul will no longer be important to me, and my love may no longer be important to him? Does it mean if I always wanted to learn or develop a musical gift or the ability to write a book, but didn't have the opportunity because of circumstances or responsibilities that it will no longer mean anything to me in the afterlife?

If love and our goals of learning, creativity and self expression or development are unimportant when I get to the Other Side, then what is important?

I felt as though my whole life and being would be nullified or negated if the things that mattered to me most in life just evaporated – were gone in the afterlife and no longer mattered.

As I wanted to remain objective and not color my answer with my own personal feelings, I asked another medium for her input regarding an answer to the same question. I feel that I was meant to get her answer because she was driving in New York City when she received my call and said she hit "reject" on her cell phone because of the traffic, but it didn't work and my call got through anyway. I hung up and when she reached her destination, she called me back. She asked her guides and replied,

> Whenever you ask different guides the same question, remember that they may have a different mindset or viewpoint than you; they may be at a different point in their evolution from you, and their reality may be different from yours. That may not be their reality. You create your own reality and the options are vast. You will express your own reality, the product of your thoughts and desires.
>
> Also remember that whatever is being channeled is being channeled through another person, and may be influenced by their prejudices or beliefs. Furthermore, the guides may have been referring to material things, which are relatively insignificant in the spirit world.

> Love is never lost. Spiritual love is very important. Trust in your own reality. Hold it in your heart.

I learned two things from this incident. One is how powerful words can be and how we must be responsible in the way we say things because of how great an impact we may have on someone. The other is that we each have our own truth. What is valuable or important to one may not be to another. Do not let the convictions of another influence you if they are significantly different from yours. Since we create very different worlds and realities for ourselves, yours may not bring happiness to me, nor mine to you.

One Hundred Nine

Collected Wisdom

I decided to take the same topics on which I have written and give a selection of comments from other books, writers and spirits on those topics that I have found to be helpful in my own learning and development. I prized and cherished these comments, which have been gathered from a variety of sources. I have included the books from which they were obtained in the bibliography.

Desires:

> We can retain some desires if they represent a deep psychological need and were unfulfilled on the earth plane. They can be fulfilled by creating an illusionary experience that will feel real to the participant.
>
> We can re-enact the strongest desires we had on earth by creating a "fantasy" through memories and imagination that will seem real to us, adapting the memory world to our desire.

If we want something we loved or didn't have in life, as long as we didn't wish to harm others, we wouldn't be denied that experience.

Everything we can imagine after death is possible to experience to some extent, if only within our own mental reality.

We serve a good God. If we need something, it would be provided for us.

The counterpart of every pure joy is here. All the joys you have will only be intensified.

God/Source

We are the reflection of the Oneness

Individuality/Personality

Consciousness of the spirit is continual.

Personality is the child of spirit and body and is never lost.

Essential nature does not change. Death is not the ticket to enlightenment. Enlightenment must happen in life or not at all.

Karma

The earth is a compressed karmic learning opportunity.

Obstacles are to be met with positive solutions.

Levels

Levels represent different energy densities.

Limitations of knowledge correlate with our stage of spiritual progression. More awareness will be given to us as we are ready for it.

Man creates his own destiny by his words, thoughts, and actions. These determine the place he will go in the afterlife. We create our own "reward" or "punishment".

We gravitate to our level of development with kindred souls.

Lies

Character is transparent. We cannot hide our true selves.

Life Lessons

The soul is a rough diamond. Its beauty is concealed until it is cut and polished.

Love/Companionship

You will find those you really love.

Tastes, outlooks, preferences, and desires determine our affinities. The law of attraction prevails. Your magnetic current draws those of similar attraction.

There is always a connection between those who love one another whether in body or spirit. There is no separation in spirit for those who love one another.

Love is the most powerful energy that exists and promotes great change.

Unconditional love comes from the mind.

In seeking the spirits of those they loved, many have found their own souls.

Oversoul

The oversoul contains our cosmic master plan, our soulprint.

Progression

Progress is advancement made by positive forward movement.

We interact with others in life for mutual progression.

We must be grateful for the chance, no matter how painful, to rise above obstacles and learn from them and incorporate that learning into the progress of our soul.

Purpose

Our purpose is learning to make more enlightened choices.

We each have a God-given intent or purpose.

We learn of evil to master and conquer our lower self.

We are put in the physical to develop the spiritual.

Reality versus Illusion

When we're in earthly form we only see a part of the picture. There lies the unreality of the material world.

Spirit is substantial, more real than the material world.

Reincarnation

We transmute the outward manifestation of our existence in conformity to the need for karmic progression. We do not undergo reincarnation, but successive continual incarnations, as we maintain form until we reunite with Source.

Sex

If you ask if there is the physical or emotional sensation of love when one is in spirit, whatever awareness is necessary for the progression of a soul in spirit will be made available to that soul.

Thought expresses the emotion.

There is a spiritualized form of affection which is higher and finer than its material counterpart.

Spirit appearance/form

We inhabit different energy sheaths. We are light inhabiting form.

In our condition our bodies are quite as solid as yours, but in as far as they are matter, they are completely under the control of mind.

Our form is more transmutable and plastic.

We are consciousness, separate existence, and maintain form until we reunite with God.

Spirit Commitment

Spiritual unions are better than the best on earth and probably eternal. We will not search without rest for completion.

At last we come into a perfect spiritual union.

Two loving souls are co-creating their own reality.

Some souls have been together for eons and eons.

There is a spiritual commitment that can be made by two loving souls in the Akashic records, and it is a powerful thing.

Spiritual Learning/Knowledge

There is an infusion of knowledge

We can have paired, shared, or observed lives.

We learn from one another, those in spirit and those in the physical. We are all each other's teachers.

Spirit Reality/Environment

The afterlife is a self-directed mental and spiritual reality.

We live on a plane of conceptual reality. We project our thoughts to create the reality we inhabit. It will seem as real to spirit as the physical world is to you.

In spirit, one creates one's own reality.

The thought forms we construct and inhabit are real to us.

The dead shape their own reality. They can also have a common, shared consensus reality.

Our experience is individual. It can be similar to the earthly experience or vastly different. It is originator dependent. We shape our surroundings to our vision. Our external reality is formed by concentrated thought.

In this invisible world there is infinite variety of conditions. The dead can only describe what they've experienced.

Your thought brings you the truth that appeals to you. Hold fast to the truth that appeals to you, for it is the truth. Never doubt that. Heaven is an unlimited space with room for many ideals.

Spirit Recall of Earth Life

One characteristic of the light body is that it will retain complete memory of its cumulative experiences.

Spirit Senses

We have the spiritual equivalent of the physical sensations not gained through the mortal organs.

Spirit can give sensation as perfectly as ever.

Emotions and sensory impressions are not as vividly felt as you ascend.

Soul Group

We dance with each other.

We assist each other's forward movement.

Ultimate Destiny

We become individualized parts of the whole with no need for expression in form.

On the 7th plane, God's laws become individualized. Interests become more personal.

One Hundred Ten

Mediumship Template

Some mediums just like to give whatever information comes through in whatever order it comes through. Other mediums like to have a set order of questions for spirit, or they devise a structured way of obtaining information. They may have a specific order in which they query the spirit for information or they may have a certain way of perceiving information.

For example, when ascertaining how a spirit died they may feel the death. They may ask the spirit to impress physical feelings on them that they felt at the time of their death. This is how some clairsentient mediums receive information. For those who are predominantly clairvoyant, the spirit may point to or darken an area of their body to indicate the site of the problem. Those who are clairaudient may hear a word, such as "heart attack".

Other mediums may devise a set of symbols unique to them. One friend of mine sees a spirit holding their hands out. If the hands are empty, they are a taker. If the hands are full, they are a giver. There is no one right way to do it. The only important thing is that the medium works out a system with their guides so that the guides and communicating spirits know what to expect and communication is more efficient, less haphazard. This is also effective in speeding up the process as what you do repetitively you get more proficient at.

Many gifted mediums develop multiple ways of perceiving the information. This is good because it gives you more to draw on, a greater arsenal of techniques, and allows you to give a more complete message.

I have devised a template for my own use combined with techniques I have learned from others, and when I am practicing discipline, I try to use it. After all, I have been told that just like in life, communication is a two way street. You shouldn't be afraid to ask the spirit questions, or to clarify a statement that you or the sitter doesn't understand.

Here is the template of questions I have devised for myself that I sometimes use. Many times I realize that different spirits have different personalities, as in life. Some are shy or reticent. Some are polite and wait for you to solicit information. Some have never communicated before and are learning the process. They may not yet be skilled at giving information. Some sitters say that mediums find it hard to read for them. Perhaps they are very private or apprehensive. Some spirits are more outgoing and loquacious. They just take over and run with it, especially if they were a talker or a good communicator in their lifetime. I found that lawyers, judges, and teachers tended to communicate very easily. I also have found out that some spirits and mediums can have a better rapport if they have a common frame of reference or are similar in personality and vibration. The more experienced you are, the less this should impact the reading you give.

Here is the template I devised for myself. It forces me to stretch myself and be consistent in how I approach the reading and get the information. It may be helpful to you if you are practicing developing your own skills, but each person must find what works best for them.

See the spirit, male or female, age and appearance

Show me image of my mother or father, grandmother or grandfather, to indicate mother or father's side and generation or

Show orb or spirit image above the sitter's shoulder, at their waist level, or at their feet for generation

Walk up a rolled out calendar for a significant year

Show calendar and highlight a spot for date

Show alphabet and highlight letters for names

Show hands on clock face for dates

or months

Show me the numbers 1 for short illness 2 long illness 3 accident 4 murder 5 suicide

Or point to area of body involved or make me feel cause of death in my body

Make me feel your personality

Show me your Interests and hobbies and career

Tell me what your living relative has been doing or significant events since you have been deceased

Give me a specific shared memory, image, fact, information, occurrence or something unique to you and the sitter that will definitely identify you and let them know that it is you or give one piece of information that will let them know that it is you specifically

Who are you with on the other side

How many children did you have and are they boys or girls

Give me a message for the sitter

Basically, I try to get:

Male or female, and appearance

Age

Cause of death

Relationship – mother's or father's side and generation, or friend, acquaintance

Whether they had spouse or children

Personality or characteristic of theirs

Interests

Career

A decade or a specific significant date, month, day, or year

A name or letter of a name

A specific object, occurrence, habit, item, or shared memory that is unique to you and the sitter that will specifically identify you (I have found this to be very helpful in identifying the spirit. It's like a light that comes on when you get a piece of information and the sitter says, "Oh, that's my husband, wife, son daughter, mother, father", and a big smile comes over their face. I have found that spirits can be very creative when giving something specific to identify themselves.)

Message for the sitter

Postscript

Is there any message you would like to leave me with?

My Guide:

> We need to be careful with our desires, because what we desire becomes manifested for us. We have the power of creation, and what is our heart's desire becomes our reality. You and I will have our own.

Harvey's Guides:

> Picture a trip you'd like to go on and it's all there for you. Don't picture death as an ending. It's a new vista, beginning, or challenge to be embraced, not feared.

I wish for my guide to have the last word.

My Guide:

> There is no one answer for everything. We learn our answers as we go along. If we ask a question, we will

be given the insight and ability to attain the answer that is right for us.

We are never alone. There are others who love us and who are waiting to share life with us on the Other Side and are helping us to navigate our course through the physical world.

Nothing that is of value is lost. Our values change as we learn. There is no person who is perfect. We all strive to be better. Don't ever give up or lose hope. There is a better life, a better way, a fulfillment. We cannot achieve perfection in the physical.

We give up on no one. Only you can give up on yourself. Help is available if we listen with our spiritual ears. There is no loss of love. We will live through the difficult times and be wiser for it. Growth can be painful but is positive. We learn to make choices that lead to happiness.

You are loved. Love is waiting and is never lost. Love is the light in our lives and the light is love. Unconditional love is forever.

Life is not easy. We can all learn if we are willing and we try. Love is forgiving and caring, and love is the light that makes our lives worthwhile.

Bibliography

Borgia, Anthony, *Life in the World Unseen*, (Kindle Edition, 2009) (Original Work Published 1954)

Cummins, Geraldine, *The Road to Immortality*, (Norfolk, England: Thetford, 1984) (Original Work Published 1932)

Cummins, Geraldine, *Beyond Human Personality,* (London, England: Psychic Press, 1935)

Cummins, Geraldine, *Travelers in Eternity,* (London, England: Knapp, Drewett & Sons, 1948)

Dresser, Charlotte & Rafferty, Fred, *Life Here and Hereafter,* (San Jose, California: Cosmos, 1927)

Dresser, Charlotte & Rafferty, Fred, *Spirit World and Spirit Life,* (Kindle Edition, 2010) (Original Work Published 1922)

Kelway-Bamber, Claude, *Claude's Book,* (New York, Henry Holt & Company, 1919)

Kelway-Bamber, L., *Claude's Second Book*, (Whitefish, Montana: Kessinger, 2010) (Original Work Published 1920)

Leadbeater, Charles, *The Mental Plane*, (London and Benares: The Theosophical Society, 1902)

Lodge, Oliver, & Lodge, Raymond, *Raymond or Life and Death, Vol. I and II*, (Kindle Edition, 2011) (Original Work Published 1916)

Marks, Jeffrey A., *The Afterlife Interviews*, Vol. I and II, (Mukitleo, Washington, Arago Press, 2013 and 2014)

Scott, John, *As One Ghost to Another*, (London, England: Spiritualist Press, 1948)

St. Clair, Shanna Spalding, *Karma I and II, (no location provided: S. C. Walter, 1993)*

Swain, Jasper, *On the Death of My Son*, (Northhamptonshire, England: The Aquarian Press, 1974)

Vogel, Gretchen, *Choices in the Afterlife*, (Keene, New Hampshire: Choices Publishing, 2010)

Winninger, Toni Ann, *Talking with Twentieth Century Men*, (Lake Bluff, Illinois: Celestial Voices, 2008)